WENDY GRANT

ARE YOU IN

Control?

A HANDBOOK FOR THOSE WHO WANT TO BE IN CONTROL OF THEIR LIVES

ELEMENT

Shaftesbury, Dorset ● Rockport, Massachusetts
Brisbane, Queensland

© Wendy Grant 1993

First published by Eastbrook Publishing in 1993

This edition published in Great Britain in 1996 by
Element Books Limited
Shaftesbury, Dorset SP7 8BP

Published in the USA in 1996 by
Element Books, Inc.
PO Box 830, Rockport, MA 01966

Published in Australia in 1996 by
Element Books Limited
for Jacaranda Wiley Limited
33 Park Road, Milton, Brisbane 4064

Illustrations by Tony Thornhill
Cover design by Max Fairbrother
Design by Roger Lightfoot
Typeset by WestKey Ltd, Falmouth, Cornwall
Printed and bound in Great Britain by
BPC Paperbacks, Aylesbury

British Library Cataloguing-in-Publication
data available

Library of Congress Cataloging-in-Publication
data available

ISBN 1–85230–778–1

Contents

Exercises

Tom
My thanks for everything

- Are there areas of your life you would like to change?
- Do you wish that you were more confident?
- Would you like to know how to improve a relationship?
- Is anger, guilt or fear spoiling the quality of your life?
- Do you want to change your responses to certain things?
- Are motivation and self-discipline a problem for you?
- Have you ever wished you knew a simple way to deal with a phobia?
- Does your memory seem to be getting worse and would you like to know how to improve it?
- Would you like to know how to use simple techniques to help you sleep well and relax completely?
- Would you like to be able to realize your full potential?

The ways to resolve these problems are simple and can be used by anyone. I have spent ten years teaching them to people and *they do work*! By writing this book I hope to make them available to all those who would truly like to be in control of their own lives.

For a number of years I have been meeting on a regular basis with a group of friends who are all qualified hypnotherapists working in private practice in the West Country. We spend a busy day together, pooling our knowledge, sharing experiences, learning from each other about things we have read and new techniques which have been tried and tested. When there is an interesting course, one of us attends, bringing back ideas and techniques that we then discuss and sometimes try out on each other.

From this wealth of experience I have put into this book those techniques that I have found most useful and effective when working with clients, or when running workshops on 'Using The Unconscious Mind'. The exercises given are not the only ways to resolve such problems, but they have been used again and again with good results by all of us.

I would particularly like to thank Patrick, Jeff and Michael for all their help, patience, support and caring. Also for the humour!

I recall one Saturday which found me leaping about in response to a chart of signs brought by Patrick, designed, supposedly, to confuse the mind and thus allow some form of instant change to take place. Tears of laughter were running down their cheeks as I finally collapsed in a heap on the settee. Ah yes! Learning to use the unconscious mind can be fun too!

Introduction

When you set out by car on an unknown journey it is obviously made easier if you carry a road map. As you travel through life it surely makes equally good sense to have a book which helps you to cope with the various problems and challenges encountered in day-to-day living.

Just as we can call out a mechanic or take the car into a garage when things go wrong, so can we visit a therapist when we don't know how to resolve emotional problems or handle our responses in certain situations. However, as many emotional and behavioural problems can be quickly and efficiently dealt with by ourselves, having a handbook telling you 'how' can often save a lot of pain, frustration, heartache and confusion.

To those who would have us believe that it is dangerous to attempt to resolve our own problems, I can only say, *We do it all the time anyway.* All problems created in the mind are resolved in the mind – they cannot be resolved anywhere else or by anyone else.

A good counsellor or therapist is able to guide you in the right direction, and his or her skills and experience can assist you in making beneficial internal changes. However, there are many times when a 'first aid kit' would enable you to take control and resolve your own problems quickly and easily.

The chances are that you would not dream of consulting a doctor or therapist if you needed help with such things as exam nerves, motivation, dealing with anger, guilt or criticism, or to help improve your performance in sport, but that some knowledge in resolving these kinds of problems would benefit you.

This then, is your 'first aid' book, designed to help you with those everyday problems that can spoil the quality of life. By using the exercises in visualization and relaxation as described, you can resolve many problems yourself – and even prevent some from ever happening.

Where drugs are prescribed to help with psychological or emotional problems, they often mask the underlying causes but cannot cure them. Surely it is far better to identify and eliminate the stress causing a headache than to take an aspirin? And how much better to set out on a difficult journey with confidence rather than take along a supply of tranquillizers.

This book can only help those people who want to take responsibility for their own lives. There are some who profess to want this but in reality find comfort from being helpless and dependent. Others find a strange fulfilling of needs by placing themselves constantly at the mercy of others – ignored as a child, it can be very satisfying to have found a way of claiming constant attention.

Although qualified therapists may find this book interesting and in some areas instructive, it is primarily written for those with little or no previous knowledge of the unconscious mind, self-hypnosis or visualization skills. I make no apology for the simplistic way in which it is written, this is deliberate.

You do not need to be academic, clever, or possess any other special abilities in order to use self-hypnosis or the visualization and relaxation techniques – all you need is the persistence to read through this book and to carry out the exercises described.

Each chapter explores and explains a subject or problem: case histories are given where appropriate to clarify points made and to help you relate to your individual problem. In all case histories, names, locations and personal details have been changed to protect the confidentiality of clients. Although not every emotional and behavioural problem is individually dealt with, the notes and examples given should be sufficient to enable you to apply them to any specific problem you may have. An exercise, where appropriate, is given in detail at the end of each chapter.

I do not profess to have all the answers, but I believe this book will help you to take control of your own life. To all my students and past clients – here is the book you asked for. From working with you I have seen the wonderful potential in all of us to use the Right Brain in a way that puts *us* in control.

To those of you whom I have never met, do give it a try; no matter how busy you are, or what the pressures may be, 15 minutes a day set aside to use the relaxation and visualization techniques described in this book will more than repay you.

1

How Your Brain Works

Everything begins and ends in the brain. From our first movements – the gasp for air, the blinking of an eye, the need to feed – to the moment we become clinically dead, the message to function at every level comes from the brain.

At first these movements, needs and functions are solely instinctual but, as we develop, the conscious and unconscious parts of the brain play an increasingly bigger role in our lives.

Over the past 30 years much research and experimentation have resulted in the recognition of the separate functions of the two halves of the brain – known as the Left Brain and Right Brain.

It has now been proven that the brain, once believed to be a single organ, is in fact two, each with many functions that cannot, under normal conditions, be done by the other. The two brains communicate or overlap by means of connecting nerve fibres (the corpus callosum). This partnership between the two brains has produced the most efficient way for us to operate and to survive.

It is not yet known whether all the functions of the brain have a usefulness relating to survival, but it is beginning to look as if this is the case.

We are not like any other animal for, in order to communicate, we rely almost entirely upon words, and we believe that no other species experiences emotions as we do.

Note: To understand those functions of the brain that are relevant to using this book we can ignore left-handedness. The same principles of the conscious and unconscious hemispheres apply here, although in some cases they may be physically reversed.

The Left Brain

The Left Brain (hemisphere) is responsible for, amongst other things, *conscious thought, logic, verbalization, critical assessment and the ability to write and think in words.*

We call the left half of the brain the conscious mind, for through it we think in words, and through conscious, verbalized thought we are made aware. Thinking in words enables us to be conscious of ourselves and our surroundings. When we awake it is not until we begin to think in words that we are aware of being.

Although not usually aware of doing so, we are constantly explaining a situation to ourselves in a way that our conscious self can understand. During most of our waking hours we operate on a verbal level, either silently or aloud.

The Right Brain

The Right Brain (hemisphere) is responsible for *emotions, creativity, intuition, dreams, imagination, visualization, and spatial vision* – in fact, all those things we cannot consciously do or control.

To perform even the simplest of tasks we appear to store

a series of tiny images in the Right Brain which we replay unconsciously when the need arises. Words are seemingly too slow and cumbersome, and tend to get stored as images. If we are unsure how to spell something, we write it down. Once this is done we are able to recognize when the word looks correct.

The Right Brain is referred to as the unconscious mind because it does not consciously, through thought awareness, do things. This does not mean that you are unconscious whilst it is in action.

Although sleep is one example of the Right Brain taking over completely, if someone suddenly bangs a door or tickles your feet you are capable of becoming immediately alert at a conscious level and making the appropriate responses.

Time is not recognized by the Right Brain – when a past emotional experience is re-stimulated it can be as powerful as if it happened yesterday. This is one of the reasons why it is impossible to use logic to resolve an emotional problem. The Right Brain is not 'reasonable'. It is, therefore, no use telling yourself or anyone else to 'forget it, it's all over' or 'it all happened years ago'.

One of the objectives of this book is to teach you how to let go of bad old feelings that no longer serve a useful function.

Overlapping

Sometimes it is necessary for the functions of the two brains to overlap. How does this work and how can we utilize it?

There are times when we need to pass a specific job to the Right Brain and then return it to the Left Brain so that we may think about it in words, verify it, and make use of the information in a conscious way.

We all do this naturally. When you are trying to recall the name of a place, person, book or film title and it's right on the tip of your tongue but you can't quite remember it, you are likely to say, 'I'll forget all about it and it will come to me in a minute'. Having made that decision you stop struggling to remember, the brain relaxes, and the information stored in the Right Brain passes through to the Left Brain and suddenly, without any apparent effort, you have the answer. It may happen in a few minutes, sometimes it may even be the next day, but the answer comes without any further conscious effort on your part. Impulses passing through the connecting nerve fibres between the Left Brain and the Right Brain allow this kind of communication to take place.

In the case of dreaming, although a dream is normally created and takes place in the Right Brain, to recall it and be able to tell someone about that dream, it is necessary to transfer the information to the Left Brain. The content of the dream can then be verbally communicated.

Artistic and creative people know intuitively when to let go of conscious verbal thought and to allow the creative Right Brain to get on with the job.

A writer will often let an idea 'incubate' at an unconscious level while doing all manner of other things to distract the conscious mind. And then, when it feels 'right', the creative writer will switch over to words and begin to put those thoughts – which seem to have manifested themselves without effort – down on paper.

The same technique is used by inventors, scientists, musicians and artists. People such as Mozart and Einstein knew the secret of using both brains to do the jobs at which they excelled.

Overlapping is essential and usually functions without us being the slightest bit aware that it is happening.

It is the Right Brain that enables us to tie a shoe lace successfully even when the Left Brain is talking about something quite different. However, to explain how we tied the shoe lace, we would have to transfer the images into words and then verbally communicate the 'how'.

Try explaining to someone how to tie a shoe lace without using images and you'll see what I mean. You'll find you *need* that overlapping – it is essential. In fact it has been going on for years without you having to pay attention to it in any way at all.

A plumber instructing an apprentice will explain verbally how and why things work, but to picture the pipes and connections he has to rely on his Right Brain activity. There is a constant 'hopping' from one hemisphere to the other as he communicates the information.

Using the Best Brain for the Job

As we grow and develop we tend to allow one or other of the brains to take over and do whatever it is capable of doing best.

The Left Brain is in control most of our waking hours, and although it does a splendid job, I believe that life is impoverished if we fail to learn how to use the Right Brain in situations where it is superior. The Right Brain can add enlightenment and enhancement to the way we live.

It seems that the Right Brain operates on a different level and is able to work either with the conscious mind or independent of it. While the Left Brain interprets words in its own conscious way, the Right Brain is busy doing exactly the same in *its* own way.

Take for example the single word 'cat'. To the Left Brain this is perceived as an animal covered with fur who miaows when it wants to be fed or let out; to the Right Brain it is likely to mean softness, warmth, a comforting feeling. If, however, your past association with cats was a bad experience, the Right Brain will react with revulsion and fear, while the Left Brain will continue to perceive it impassively as an animal covered with fur.

Although interpreting the Right Brain's responses in words is done by the Left Brain, the emotions remain strictly Right Brain responses.

Conscious or Unconscious?

When we are not able to put thoughts into words it does not follow that we become unconscious. A small baby lying in a pram, watching the leaves of a tree moving in the breeze, is not aware consciously of what is happening – he has yet to learn a verbal language. He must rely upon his visual and sensual responses. The baby is, at this stage, very much Right Brain orientated, following and responding to the facial expressions of his mother, her tone of voice, her touch and smell. As the baby becomes familiar with words and can interpret the message behind those words, the Left Brain becomes more and more dominant and the sensual and visual responses diminish.

We now know that even under anaesthetic, we are not totally unconscious. Medical research has revealed that suggestions given to people in this state are heard, stored, and responded to when they return to full consciousness.

In a London hospital an experiment was carried out on a number of women undergoing hysterectomies. An audio cassette was played to half of them telling them that the operation was for their future well-being, that they would recover completely and soon be in excellent health. Those who heard this message did actually recover more quickly and were able to leave hospital two to three days ahead of those who had not heard the cassette.

Note: To avoid preconditioning, the women were not told which of them would be hearing the cassette during the operation.

Using the Right Brain to Make Change

Having learned how to access the unconscious mind, it can be used constructively for change. When the critical conscious mind is bypassed, suggestion is accepted by the unconscious mind and becomes a belief.

It is important to understand that the Right Brain works from emotion-based concepts whereas the Left Brain uses logic and reason. Where there is conflict the emotions almost always win. You may set out thinking you have control, and even for a while manage to sustain that control, but ultimately the emotions manifest themselves and take over. No matter how many times you may tell yourself that spiders are harmless, if you have a spider phobia and one runs across your hand, you will either leap up and thrust it from you or freeze with horror.

The unconscious mind does not stop to work things out logically – when it feels threatened (for whatever reason) it immediately goes into action. It does not stop and ask if, in this situation, it needs to react in this way.

The good news is that by understanding how the Right Brain works you can utilize it to change your responses where they are no longer required in a survival situation.

You can use your image-making ability (the imagination) positively to build confidence and self-esteem instead of allowing it to destroy those feelings.

You can use visualization to undo phobic responses, strengthen resolve and motivation, and improve learning skills.

By understanding such responses as anger, guilt, jealousy and over-indulgence, you can train your Right Brain to work constructively in resolving those problems.

Visualization and positive suggestion can assist your own natural healing processes and improve the immune system.

Whew! Don't worry if all that seems a lot to take in. But

you will have absorbed a great deal at an unconscious level just by reading this. Remember, the Right Brain can, and does, work for you, usually with no conscious effort on your part.

2

Self-Hypnosis

Hypnosis

What is hypnosis? One definition describes it as 'an altered state of conscious awareness'. I think this is an excellent definition, for at no time during hypnosis does one become semi-conscious or unconscious. There is certainly nothing artificial or unnatural about being in a state of hypnosis.

Disregard all films or stage performances you have seen that portrayed the hypnotist having total power over the subject, because *you can never be hypnotized against your will*. You can never, through hypnosis or by suggestion, be made to violate your own values or standards of behaviour.

All hypnosis is self-hypnosis. The hypnotist, using his skills, will verbally guide you into that state known as hypnosis, but only you can make it happen by following the hypnotist's instructions and responding to what he says.

But, you may say, you have seen or heard of people who, under instructions from the stage hypnotist, jumped on a table and danced, barked like a dog, or crowed like a cock. Well, if you were likely to do any of these things under the influence of alcohol, then you might be persuaded into doing them under hypnosis. What hypnosis does, is to enable you to enter a very pleasant, mentally-relaxed state where your inhibitions no longer seem to limit or control you.

How Does Hypnosis Work?

The brain works by producing impulses known as brainwaves. Like an electric current, these alter in frequency depending on what we are doing.

For most of the time, when we are asleep, the brain produces a gentle, slow rhythm of impulses known as theta brainwaves; these change and become erratic when we dream. When we awake the brain becomes much more active and produces impulses known as beta brainwaves.

Somewhere between sleep and wakefulness are those impulses known as alpha brainwaves; these occur when we are daydreaming, when we get involved in a good book or film, or perhaps when we are driving down a familiar road and we let our minds wander. Before we go to sleep and as we awake we produce alpha brainwaves. *Alpha brainwaves are perfectly normal – they occur in everyone.*

At alpha level we become very receptive to change and suggestion. The skilled hypnotherapist guides you into this state and then uses positive suggestions to help you make changes that are beneficial to your happiness and well-being.

By using words, the hypnotherapist draws your attention to various feelings and responses you are experiencing. Sometimes these are physical – the touch of your hand against the chair, the rhythm of your breathing, the warmth of your skin, a loss or strengthening of feelings; sometimes she will draw your awareness to sounds or smells which were already there, and yet until that moment you had not noticed them. All this helps you to have a belief in the therapist and to follow her suggestions.

A very good example of how you go naturally to alpha level occurs when you are watching television. If the film is sad, funny or frightening, you are likely to respond emotionally (most of us will confess to the occasional tear in response to a sad film). To enable you to enjoy the story of the film, you allow the conscious, logical Left Brain to relax. As it closes down, your imagination takes over and you begin to respond emotionally to the film. But you know very well that if the telephone rang you would be able to get up and answer it – you would still be in control.

If, during this experience, your Left Brain had stayed in control, you would probably have said, 'They are only acting it, it's not for real' – and you would not have been able to enjoy the film to the same extent.

Self-Hypnosis

Self-hypnosis occurs when we learn to relax *deliberately* to alpha level and can recognize that we have achieved that level. We can then use our own suggestions and visualization to resolve personal problems, and to strengthen, mould and improve various areas of our lives.

Once a positive suggestion has been received by the unconscious mind it will be put into effect. That's the way the brain works!

Can Anyone be Hypnotized?

Anyone who can concentrate and follow simple instructions can enter this alpha state. Some people learn more quickly and easily than others, and about 10 per cent of the population are *very* 'hypnotizable'.

Small children and mentally disabled people do not

usually respond to conventional hypnosis, either because they are incapable of following instructions or their concentration span is too short. Having said this, I feel I should point out how easily a baby can be lulled into the alpha state by gentle rocking, rhythmic caressing, or the sounds of a lullaby.

The ability to go into a deep hypnotic state is not required, or even beneficial, for self-hypnosis. You need to remain sufficiently aware so that you can follow instructions you have learned or read, and use visualization techniques. Should you go very deeply into hypnosis you would simply stop doing these things – it wouldn't do any harm but it wouldn't achieve the desired results.

This only applies to self-hypnosis. When a hypnotherapist is working with you, you may stop thinking in words and even believe that you went to sleep for a while. The suggestions and words used while you are in this deeply relaxed state will still be accepted and acted upon.

Using an audio cassette can have the same effect. You may relax so deeply you actually *do* go to sleep – but you will not become deaf! You will still hear and respond to the recorded words.

If you suffer from epilepsy it is advisable to consult your doctor before seeking the help of a qualified hypnotherapist. However, I see no reason why you cannot use the relaxation and visualization exercises described in this book as they are quite natural to all of us.

No one can stop us using our imagination. But, unfortunately, it is often used to imagine the worst possible scenario! So many people picture disaster or making a mess of things, quite unconsciously programming themselves for failure.

Fortunately, you can learn to use the power of the mind and the influence of your imagination in a beneficial way. That is what this book is all about!

Are There Any Side Effects?

Using self-hypnosis is very much like relaxing and picturing things inside your mind just before going to sleep. If you are already tired when doing this you may become so relaxed that you slip quite naturally into sleep, that is all.

No one has ever been 'stuck' in hypnosis. No one, to my knowledge, has ever become dependent upon it. And every report that I have received from clients and students confirms that it is a very pleasant and rewarding experience.

How Can Hypnosis Help?

Hypnosis can help by enabling you to identify problems and mental blocks. In this relaxed state you are better able to understand your emotional responses and behaviour in certain situations.

During self-hypnosis you can reprogramme your responses. You can choose the way in which you want to behave, and strengthen your will with positive suggestions.

Using visualization at alpha level you are able to 'stand back' and observe yourself and 'see' how you can make changes. This form of mental relaxation helps you to release your creativity without interference from the conscious Left Brain.

Self-hypnosis can help you to realize your full potential.

Using the Exercises

Before doing the exercises, make sure that you are in a warm, comfortable, relaxed position where you will not be interrupted. The children yelling for their tea or the cat suddenly leaping on your stomach are not conducive to a successful session of self-hypnosis. If you can find nowhere to be on your own for ten minutes, lock yourself in the loo – at least the chances are no one will disturb you there!

When you come to an exercise, read through it several times to familiarize yourself with the procedure, then put the book aside and, following the steps given, work your way through the exercise.

If you find that you become so relaxed that you fall asleep while doing the exercises, you may like to make a recording of them. You can then listen to the cassette as you relax and respond. It is necessary, when you record for the purpose of self-hypnosis, to use a voice without any highs or lows – a soft rhythmic voice is best.

As an alternative, you may ask a trusted friend or relative to slowly read the exercise to you whilst you relax and respond. When doing this, ensure that the reader leaves pauses where indicated by the dots – these are to give you time to respond and to allow for visualization to have effect.

Visual techniques to help you achieve alpha level are given at the end of the book, but we will start here with one of my favourites.

Make sure that you are in a warm, comfortable, relaxed position.

Exercise 1 – Learning to Achieve Self-Hypnosis

1 Gently close your eyes and take a deep, deep breath, really fill your lungs with air then breathe out and relax . . . Continue breathing deeply and evenly and as you do so notice any jerkiness or unevenness in your breathing and try to smooth it out . . .

2 As you continue breathing deeply and evenly, imagine that each breath you take in is like a swing going up into the air, and as you exhale the swing comes back down again . . .

3 Mentally create your surroundings. Your swing can be in any place you choose: in a familiar garden or one from your own imagination; it can be in a park or tied to a tree in an old orchard . . . You may like to imagine you are a child again, sitting on the swing, or perhaps you are pushing someone else . . . As you continue breathing deeply in and out, imagine what you can see as you look up . . . a clear blue sky overhead with an aeroplane high above you, its wings shining silver in the sunlight. Perhaps you hear birds or the sound of children's voices as they play. As the swing goes up you may be able to see over the treetops or rooftops and you may see a church spire in the distance . . .

4 Now as you continue breathing deeply and evenly, notice any physical discomfort: it may be in your lower back, in your neck, or your shoulders . . . When you have located it, calmly acknowledge it . . . and as you continue to breathe deeply in and out, imagine that you are feeding oxygen directly to that area – life-giving oxygen, cleansing and healing – and as you breathe out you release any stress or tension, you just let it melt away . . .

5 Continue in this way for a few minutes until you feel

comfortably relaxed and then begin to mentally check over your body, starting with your feet. Think of each toe in turn, first on one foot and then on the other . . . By now you will notice that you have become so relaxed that you can hardly feel some of your toes at all and that you can barely distinguish one toe from the next . . . Be aware of the feelings of heaviness in your legs as you let go and relax. Let them feel heavy, so heavy, so comfortable and so relaxed. That's fine, just let every muscle go on and on relaxing as you continue checking over your body . . . Feel your stomach muscles relax as you breathe gently in and out . . . Notice the rhythm of your breathing . . . it has slowed down and that's perfectly natural, the same thing happens each night as you go to sleep . . . You may even be able to feel your heart beating as you relax deeper and deeper. Let your scalp relax. Allow all of the muscles in your face, your mouth and lips to relax. Let the muscles in your neck and shoulders feel soft and relaxed . . . Now let any stress or tension from your head, neck and shoulders flow down your arms and out through the tips of your fingers . . . Notice your arms begin to feel heavy, so heavy and so comfortable as you let go and relax . . . notice now the feelings and sensations in your hands and fingers . . . be aware of any tingling, any throbbing of pulses, any warmth or coldness . . .

6 Be still and breathe quietly . . . Be aware of your own feelings . . . Each one of us experiences this level of relaxation – the alpha level – in our own way. For some it is a feeling of great heaviness in the legs, arms, or in the body; others experience a weightless floating sensation. You may feel that your feet are numb or you may experience a tingling sensation. You are simply learning to recognize total relaxation, and with practice you will be able to achieve this state quickly and easily. In this

lovely relaxed way you begin to recognize your own feelings and sensations. Note these physical signals for they tell you when you have reached the level of relaxation necessary for positive instructions and suggestions to be received by your unconscious mind.

7 You are now ready to give yourself positive instructions and suggestions. Begin by using short simple sentences. Say quietly to yourself, *I am relaxed . . . I'm feeling fine . . . I can use self-hypnosis to improve my life.* Repeat these statements several times.

8 For a few minutes enjoy this lovely experience of total relaxation. Feel good about yourself. Feel optimistic about your future. Think for a few moments about your past achievements – from the moment when you first stood up on your own, wobbled, sat down, got up again, and from there learned to walk. Perhaps you can recall the first time you wrote your own name, the first time you rode a bike or learned to swim. The day you started school. Think of the many things you have achieved . . . by the age of two or three you had learned to speak and understand a language.

9 Count slowly backwards from five to one and as you do so open your eyes and return to full conscious awareness. Look around the room, have a good stretch and feel pleased with your success so far.

Note: When you use self-hypnosis in bed at night it is not necessary to alert yourself afterwards; you can allow yourself to drift down quite naturally into your normal state of sleep.

For the next few days try to practise this first exercise at least once a day. Become really familiar with the procedure.

When you feel ready to apply your own words in a positive way to a specific problem, substitute them for the ones that I have given at step 7. This might take the form of wanting to be confident at a job interview, in which case you would say something like, *I will attend the interview with confidence . . . I am going to enjoy the experience . . . I will be relaxed, calm, and in control.* Then visualize yourself behaving in the way in which you want to present yourself. Allow the calm, confident feelings to be really experienced.

Don't start worrying about how 'deeply' you go into hypnosis – it really doesn't have any effect on the result.

Remember, *once a positive suggestion has been accepted by your unconscious mind it will be put into effect.*

This isn't a race; if it takes a little longer than you expected to reach alpha level it really doesn't matter. You are learning something new that will equip you for life.

With practice you will succeed. No one can measure what is going on inside your unconscious mind. By merely reading these words you are already absorbing and responding at a level that will in time delight and surprise you.

3

You and Your Imagination

Imagination – What is It?

Let's call imagination your capacity for creating images in your mind – your 'image-making ability'. In order to use your imagination constructively you need to realize that it is capable of doing far more than creating fantasy situations. Apart from picturing such scenes as missing your bus, losing your job, or falling off a ladder, you can create any kind of picture or series of pictures that you choose.

Your imagination rules your world. Without the ability to create in pictures, the car would never have been invented, advances would not have been made in medicine and surgery and electricity would not be utilized in the thousands of ways we now take for granted.

Unfortunately the imagination can also hold back or inhibit our lives, often with disastrous results. Take, for example, a man who imagines his wife is having an affair with someone. In his mind scenes develop until he is convinced that this affair is a reality. He becomes so incensed by these pictures and the resulting emotions, that he goes out and kills the man whom he 'sees' as the secret lover.

Those who have a fear of flying may picture the plane crashing and this prevents them from ever travelling by air.

Imagined ridicule or criticism can prevent a person from ever attempting anything new.

You are, by now, probably able to think of something that, though only imagined, has prevented you from achieving something you would like to be able to do.

Using Your Imagination Constructively

When you realize how much you do use your imagination, you will at once begin to change your concept of things. You will see how, by using your imagination positively, you can put yourself in control of most situations.

Many people believe they have poor visualization, they cannot readily conjure up pictures of leafy country lanes or golden sandy beaches. Nevertheless we all do unconsciously create pictures in our mind and we can, with practice, learn to do so at will.

For a moment pause and picture your own front door. What colour is it? How high is it? Where exactly is the door knob or key hole? Which way does it open? What is the first thing you see as you step inside? This simple exercise should demonstrate to you how readily and frequently you use your visual ability.

We picture everything, most of it quite unconsciously. We would never find our way home if we did not recognize landmarks such as streets, houses and trees. I am quite sure you do not have to stop and read the name of your road, or the number of your house when you arrive there, to confirm that that is where you live! In your mind there is a very clear picture of what your home looks like and you instantly recognize it.

If you mislay something, you will, quite naturally, reconstruct your actions, replaying them in your mind in order to help you picture where you left your glasses, book, or tool.

Apart from your ability to hold and recall visual information, you can actually change the way you feel about things by deliberately altering and moving the pictures in your mind. Doing this is the key to change and control.

Changing Images

We all carry around inside our heads an image of the way we see ourselves. People who are very confident and self-assured have a very positive image of who they are and how they appear to others. Shy, retiring people operate their 'image-making capacity' in reverse; they see themselves as unimportant, unattractive, foolish and uninteresting, and they have a very poor, negative picture of themselves.

By changing the internal image of yourself you will begin to respond to that new image. We could not survive without this ability to change images. Some people, however, do find it extremely difficult to 'grow up' and make changes. They pass through life continuing to behave like a spoilt or demanding child. They have learned a behaviour pattern which once worked for them, and have never made the transition from seeing themselves as small and helpless to mature and adult.

Picturing in advance how you would cope positively in a threatening or difficult situation, will equip you to deal with it should it happen. Picturing yourself collapsing in such a situation is a programme for disaster.

Placing Images

Recognizing that you can create pictures in your mind will enable you to progress to the next step: changing the position of images inside your head.

Although you may not have noticed it, when you visualize things or situations you place them in different positions.

Pause and think for a few minutes about what you did last Christmas. Where were you when you awoke? Who was the first person to greet you?

Most likely you will find that those pictures in your mind are to the left. This is so for the majority of us. But for some people, reconstructed scenes may be to the right, up or down. We all have our own way of positioning those things we visualize, and by recognizing where we place our own images we can begin to use this knowledge to make changes. For things that happened long ago, the images are most often way off to the left, and for future happenings (like sitting an exam or going on holiday next summer) they are usually positioned to the right. Events that are currently taking place are most often seen directly in front of us.

Watch someone being interviewed on television and you will notice that their eyes are constantly moving as they respond to the questioning.

Now take a few minutes off and discover where you picture things. Think about several happenings . . . past, present and future.

If you experienced any difficulty in doing this, don't worry! You have just become too consciously aware of the process to do it naturally. You have told yourself that you want to have this piece of information at a conscious level; the next time it occurs naturally you will be able to 'see' where you place your images.

This knowledge can be used very effectively in helping to let go of unpleasant memories. We do have a tendency to keep old unwanted experiences alive by placing them directly in front of us when we recall them. This makes them still feel very real and creates strong emotional responses. By deliberately and gradually moving the picture/s round to the back of your head when you think of them, you really can let go. Letting go of the past and putting it behind you is exactly what you are doing.

Moving images can also be used very effectively to motivate yourself (more about this later).

Recalling Information

You have read it, seen it, or been a part of it – but you just can't quite remember the details you wish to recall! But once you know where you place past events inside your head, you can turn your eyes in that direction and, in a relaxed way, reconstruct the situation. (*Note:* It is always easier to do visual exercises at alpha level, and with your eyes closed.)

Ask someone to think about something they have been putting off doing. Watch their eyes and you will see them move in a certain direction. It is almost as if what they have been putting off is stored away in a cupboard and they pull it out and look at it. Talking about 'putting off' doing something takes on a completely new meaning when you recognize this is how the brain operates. It does seem to 'put off to one side' the things it does not want to deal with.

Once you recognize your own way of positioning pictures in your mind, you can use the knowledge to your advantage.

A Different Kind of Language

Much is now written and spoken about body-language, but it is not often recognized how the words we use indirectly express 'what' and 'how' we are feeling or seeing something. 'Tough', 'hard', 'dig that', 'tread softly', tell us of someone who experiences many things through physically feeling; the words 'picture', 'light', 'dark tunnel', 'path', 'beautiful' indicate a very visual person. 'Loud', 'crashing', 'like music', would be words used by people tuned-in to sound when expressing themselves or describing something.

Recognizing this 'word' language and using a similar word structure to that of the person with whom we wish to communicate, enables us to gain a much better rapport. Many people do this quite naturally – and we usually feel almost instantly at ease with them.

In a way it is all very exciting, and as we become aware of these things it opens up new perceptions and understanding.

Case History

The headmaster of a school came to see me 'I haven't a real problem,' he told me. 'Normally I'm very confident. In fact I can get up and speak in front of a thousand parents and it doesn't bother me at all. But I can't get up on the dance floor, and my wife would really like me to take her dancing sometimes.'

When he pictured himself dancing, he always created a scene in which he was 'making a fool of himself'. I explained how he could move these pictures around inside his head. He experimented with this idea for a few minutes and then moved the negative images until he managed (his own words) 'to slip them behind my head'. He was then able to create new, clear, satisfactory images of himself at dancing school, learning from scratch how to do things properly.

A couple of years later I met him and he told me, with some pride, that he and his wife had recently been awarded gold medals for ballroom dancing.

Exercise 2 – Changing Images

Remember! Always read right through an exercise first, familiarize yourself with the procedure, and then put aside this book and do the exercise. You can put the exercise on an audio cassette if you wish – you would then simply relax, listen and respond.

1 Gently close your eyes and take a deep, deep breath . . . really fill your lungs with air and then breathe out and relax. Continue breathing deeply and evenly, and as you do so notice any jerkiness or unevenness in your breathing and try to smooth it out . . .

2 As you continue breathing deeply and evenly, imagine that each breath you take in is like a swing going up into the air, and as you exhale the swing comes back down again . . .

3 Mentally create your surroundings. Your swing can be in any place you choose: in a familiar garden or one from your own imagination, it may be in a park or tied to a tree in an old orchard . . . You may like to imagine you are a child again sitting on the swing, or perhaps you are pushing someone else . . . As you continue breathing deeply in and out, imagine what you can see as you look up . . . a clear blue sky overhead with an aeroplane high above you, its wings shining silver in the sunlight. Perhaps you hear birds or the sound of children's voices as they play. You may be able to see over the tops of the trees, you may see roof tops or a distant church spire . . .

4 As you continue breathing deeply and evenly notice any physical discomfort – it may be in your lower back, in your neck or shoulders . . . When you have located it, calmly acknowledge it . . .

5 Now as you breath in, imagine that you are feeding oxygen directly to that area – life-giving oxygen, cleansing and healing – and as you breathe out you release any stress or tension, you just let it melt away

6 Continue in this way for a few minutes until you feel comfortably relaxed . . . Now begin mentally to check over your body, starting with your feet. Think of each toe in turn, first on one foot and then on the other . . . By this time you will notice that you can hardly feel some of your toes at all, and that you can barely distinguish one toe from the next . . . Be aware of the feelings in your legs as you let go and relax. Let them feel very, very heavy. That's fine, just let them go on and on relaxing . . . Continue checking over your body, your stomach muscles, your chest, your back . . . Notice the rhythm of your breathing . . . it has slowed down. You may even be able to feel your heart beating as you let go and relax. Let your scalp relax . . . allow all of the muscles in your face, your mouth and lips to relax. Let your neck and shoulders relax and as you do so imagine all the stress and tension from your head, neck, and shoulders flowing down your arms and out through the tips of your fingers. Your arms begin to feel heavy, so heavy and comfortable as you relax deeper and deeper. Notice now the feelings and sensations in your hands and fingers . . . be aware of any tingling, any throbbing of pulses, any warmth or coldness. Recognize your own signals telling you that you are relaxed and that you are at alpha level.

7 In this relaxed state think of a situation in which you see yourself *not* performing well. This may be going for a job interview, speaking in public, sticking up for your rights in a shop, taking part in some sport, or whatever comes to mind . . . Picture this on a television screen. Make this picture as real and alive as you can.

Imagine using the controls to add colour and sound. Bring it into sharp focus. Perhaps you are looking hot and bothered, or pathetic. How do you see yourself in that situation?

8 Give this picture a title. See it now in vivid colour on the screen, with your name. It may say, for example, JOHN SMITH TAKING HIS DRIVING TEST, or MIRIAM GRANT SPEAKING IN PUBLIC.

9 You now press a button on the control panel in your hand and there appears in the top right-hand corner of the screen – superimposed over the other picture – a small picture of you the way you would like to present or conduct yourself in this situation. This tiny picture, like a passport photo, shows the way you want to be. To start with, this picture of the 'future you' will not be too clear; it may not even be in colour yet, but that's okay, in a few minutes you are going to change all that.

10 Still watching the screen, you press another button on the controls and the tiny picture grows bigger and brighter until it fills the frame, completely obliterating the original picture of the 'old you'. And now the title is different. Between your name and your goal are the words SUCCESSFULLY ACHIEVES (or COMPLETES).

Note: If you are using this exercise to help you feel confident about a job interview, you would have the words in vivid colour above the positive-outcome picture of yourself – for example, JANET BROWN SUCCESSFULLY COMPLETES HER JOB INTERVIEW.

11 Open your eyes for a moment . . . Now close them again. Repeat this visualization, starting with the picture of the 'old you' that you want to change. Again you press a button and in the top right-hand corner

there appears the little picture of you the way you want to be. Press again and the tiny 'future you' picture fills the frame. Repeat this visualization exercise several more times and as you do so, you will notice that the original picture of you – the 'old you' – becomes fainter and less real, while the new picture becomes brighter and clearer. Stop with the new positive picture of yourself on the screen and feel yourself respond to that new image. Focus for a few moments on your name and the word SUCCESSFULLY.

12 Count slowly backwards from five to one and as you do so open your eyes and return to full conscious awareness. Look around the room, have a good stretch and feel pleased with your success so far.

Note: Pausing and thinking occasionally for a few moments about your new image and positive feelings will enable you to make the changes that you want to make.

You can repeat this exercise at any time you feel the need, and you can use it to deal with as many different situations as you wish.

This visual exercise can be applied to any situation where poor self-image is causing you problems and/or preventing you from doing something you very much want to do, or ought to be able to do.

Case History

Mike, a mechanic, came to see me because he had developed dermatitis and his doctor had suggested that he should change his job to get away from oil, grease and strong cleaning materials. But Mike loved his work and was searching for another way to resolve his skin problem.

Using hypnosis I asked him to visualize himself at

the gym he frequently used. I suggested that he imagined himself taking a shower after working-out and then to see his reflection in a mirror with his skin perfectly healthy. I asked him to tell me how he felt when he looked at that image. He felt fine. I then asked him to imagine stepping into that image and to imagine how it felt to have a skin free from any disorder. Again he said it felt fine. At this point I confirmed that he could, if he chose to, keep his skin that way and still have his job as a mechanic.

Two weeks later he returned and his skin had completely cleared.

About 18 months later he came to see me once more, this time because he wanted to learn to use self-hypnosis to assist with his sport. He told me that despite continuing with his work as a garage mechanic, the dermatitis had never returned.

4

Understanding Yourself

Why Does it Happen?

Why do I let it happen? Why do I always allow other people to push me around? Why do I feel I've always got to try and please everybody? Why do I think everyone else can do things better than I can? Why do I always anticipate things going wrong? Why do I lose my temper at the slightest provocation? Why can't I answer back? Why do I feel inferior?

These are some of the questions I get asked when lecturing to groups or talking to clients. They are angry with themselves, often despairing; many are fed-up with the way they are conducting their lives. They are looking for some kind of magic to change them. 'Using my will-power just doesn't seem to work,' they tell me.

But there are solutions to these behavioural patterns and responses that have become a burden. The answer lies in the Right Brain.

Why Logic Doesn't Work

You cannot overcome emotional responses and uncon-scious behaviour patterns by using logic or common sense.

No amount of willpower can consistently override bad feelings.

Being told to 'pull yourself together' or to 'get a hold of yourself' will not work because the reasoning part of your brain (the Left Brain) has nothing to do with feelings.

Using the conscious mind to understand the processes leading to a problem is useful and enlightening, but does not offer a cure or solution.

Struggling to contain powerful, emotional, bad feelings and to control stress consciously, results in the body becoming ill in some way or, at the very least, causes depletion of the immune system – as most medical people now acknowledge.

The body is like a machine: put it under too much stress and something breaks down. In the case of a machine, a fuse may blow, a spring break or a bolt shear. Under pressure, human beings experience migraines, stomach ulcers, repeated bouts of 'flu or the 'flare up' of an old complaint. If the body holds out then the mind may say, *that's enough*, and feelings of depression, insomnia and excessive anxiety are experienced.

There is *always* a reason for everything. You have not become weak, useless, hopeless, spineless, self-conscious, acutely embarrassed, a defeatist – or however else you may see yourself – without a long process of happenings that have contributed to making you that way. Your reactions and responses are as a result of what has happened to you. *They are not your fault!*

Because emotions are based in the Right Brain, any change to our emotional responses must be made there. The Left Brain cannot change the way we feel.

Conditioning

Every one of us is conditioned by our upbringing. The ways in which we are taught, disciplined, or shown by example, all contribute towards making us the person we are.

We are born with certain characteristics and have a tendency towards a certain personality. Even identical twins will have their own individual personalities and ways of coping with life – one may be adventurous, confident and outgoing, while the other may be reserved, timid, unsure, hiding behind the behaviour of his twin.

To a great extent these inherent characteristics can be encouraged, strengthened, used constructively, exploited or overcome by those involved in our development. If we are told often enough that we are stupid, wrong, useless or shy, then we grow to believe it. We produce a behavioural pattern to support that belief and we really think of it as our own.

Most learned responses come through our development within the home or school.

Small children naturally want to explore their world, to experiment, and to experience things. This is where the first conflict usually begins. Parents, on seeing their baby

We are conditioned by our upbringing.

attempting something that they consider dangerous, intervene in order to protect the child. Often there is an overreaction, even punishment, in an endeavour to keep control.

This isn't a crime. This isn't a case of bad parents trying to stifle natural instincts in the child struggling to discover the world around him. Usually the discipline or control is motivated by love, or fear.

It seems strange that no one is given any training in how to be a good parent, and few of us study the psychology behind parenthood before we find ourselves thrown in at the deep end.

The natural learning process – which in a close-knit community was passed down – has all but disappeared because of the way in which we now live. Even those grandparents who are available to advise or instruct often hesitate to do so. Things seem to have changed so much that they are afraid lest their values and experiences are labelled wrong, bad or, at best out-dated.

As parents we do our best, but what we see as best may not necessarily be seen as such from the viewpoint of the child. Reacting against parental discipline, the child may become angry, desperate, frustrated. Some children eventually become afraid to try anything new for fear of disapproval. Praise and approval are as essential to the development of a child as are food and drink. Children thrive and blossom in an environment where they feel good about themselves and are given encouragement in what they attempt.

Now let your mind drift back. Think of a time when, as a child, you experienced conflict – perhaps there was something you wished to attempt, or to be part of, and your parents (or the person responsible for you at that time) tried to dissuade you. They may have actively opposed you, or forbade you to do that thing – even scaring you or punishing you in order to prevent it.

Did you continue with that action, risking the consequences? Or did you abandon your quest and try to please, to gain approval? If the parent or teacher's disapproval was strong enough, you probably gave up. If so, did you feel frustrated, disappointed, or relieved?

Maybe it was easy for you; perhaps pleasing mattered most. One of our greatest fears as children is of love being withdrawn. *Mummy won't love you if . . .* or *You will make Daddy cross if . . .* is often sufficient to stop most small children from continually pushing against the restraint they encounter.

Okay, so all this helped you to survive; after all, you had to continue to live with these people, you didn't want a hard time. But as you grew up, as you tried to become an individual, separating yourself from the security of the family, other fears may have begun to creep in. These fears, not usually recognized at a conscious level, began to make you feel bad about certain things.

Change, except for the most adventurous, is often painful. Situations such as going to school for the first time, standing up in class and reading aloud, moving from junior to senior school, making your first visit to the doctor or dentist on your own, all present change and can be very frightening.

Risking failure or ridicule is one of our deepest fears. We need desperately to feel 'one of the crowd' – to be accepted, to conform – and this enables us to feel safe. This is one of the reasons why bullying – being made to feel different or an outsider – is so hard to bear: our very existence feels threatened.

Another problem that young people growing towards independence often have to cope with is the inability of a parent to let go. In the case of a mother, having a child need her can become essential to her own survival; it is seen as a reflection of her own worth. Unconsciously she does everything she can to hold on to the child. This will often make the child so psychologically dependent that when the mother eventually dies, the child simply cannot cope and ends up as a depressive or lives in a constant state of anxiety. In a number of cases such a situation leads, sadly, to suicide.

The mother's fear may manifest itself in subtle ways: *I shouldn't do that dear, you might hurt yourself. Stay here with Mummy* – so the child watches the other children climbing the slide in the park while he/she stays 'safely' on the grass. Somewhere in the child's mind the thought begins to take root that being safe means not venturing forth with the other children.

The mother overheard saying, *She's afraid to let me out of her sight*, is presenting an indirect suggestion that is hard to resist. The child may not have been afraid, but now doubt has been planted. Was there perhaps some unknown 'thing' that would 'get her' if she lost sight of Mummy for a moment?

You need me to do that for you, is another seemingly innocent statement that can have a profound effect. Said often enough, the recipient really believes it. Going off to school camp with the other children then becomes a terrifying thought, and attempting to cook his/her own dinner or make his/her own bed, becomes an overwhelming task.

Discipline is also important and necessary for the stability of a child. Recent research has shown that those who lacked discipline as children find it far harder to cope and have many more problems than those who were brought up with rules that had to be obeyed.

Discipline enables children to feel safe: they know how far they can go. Discipline also says, *I care about you and because of this I can't let you do as you please*. When discipline is fair and just, children recognize this and, although they may protest loudly on occasions, instinctively know it is for their own good.

I have met many people who have come to me because they recognize that the way they are behaving is spoiling their lives. These are the sort of things they say to me: *I'd love to apply for a different job but it involves speaking up in front of others and I could never do that . . . I'm quite helpless on my own . . . I'd love to go abroad for a holiday but I dare not fly . . . I feel so self-conscious it's ruining my life.* Do they need to feel this way? The answer is No, but they don't know how to change and they are trapped by their own limiting beliefs.

Case History

A woman once told me how she longed to be able to assert herself. She wanted to stop feeling that she always had to please everyone else – even her own children!

I asked what would have happened if she had attempted to assert herself when she was young. A look of horror spread across her face. 'We wouldn't have dared to,' she said. 'Not with a father like ours!'

The way she saw it, pleasing her father had been an essential ingredient to her survival. She could not, even as an adult, bear to contemplate the results of what would have happened had she opposed him.

Now, although her husband was in no way similar to her father, and she knew that she had nothing to fear from him, she could not stop herself from behaving in the same way that had appeased her father. By so doing she avoided the slightest risk of anger or confrontation. Pleasing everyone was her way of feeling safe. But she did not like herself for this and there was a lot of internal anger and frustration directed at her own (as she saw it) weakness.

If she had been content to go on behaving in the same old way she would not have had a problem (though I doubt it would have been good for her children), but she wanted to be free to choose her own responses.

By learning to use self-hypnosis and positive visualization she gradually built up her sense of self-worth and set about making those changes that were important to her.

Programmed to Survive

Survival is our primary function. Above all else we are programmed to survive. Going back to our beginnings, when human beings lived in primitive conditions – in caves or stone huts – being able to run away or fight was essential to survival. There wasn't much else one could do when confronted by a lion or tiger in search of its dinner!

The survival part of our unconscious mind recognizes a life-threatening situation long before we recognize it consciously. The brain sends messages to the body causing it immediately to set about producing the ideal conditions to cope with the 'flight or fight' situation. The heart-beat increases, a surge of adrenaline provides a boost to speed and strength, the digestive system closes down, and energy is directed to where it is most needed. All these activities ensure that the body survives.

That was fine when we lived in primitive conditions, and this 'flight or fight' response is still necessary and used by us in life-threatening situations. Nothing should be attempted to override this – it helps us to stay alive.

However, in a civilized society, we are rarely, if ever, confronted by such life-threatening situations. The trouble is that the part of the brain responsible for setting this survival system in operation does not use logic or reason; it goes on responding in its programmed way when we feel threatened, even when this is not in our best interests.

What happens, for example, when you reach the check-out at the supermarket and discover you have mislaid your purse or wallet and the person standing behind you is getting very impatient? You begin to feel all eyes are on you and you experience that terrible feeling of being isolated from the rest of humanity. *You feel threatened*. You want to abandon the shopping and run from the store. Embarrassed, aware that you are not behaving in the accepted manner, it becomes one of those moments when you wish the ground would open up and swallow you. Repeated visits to the store (or to a similar one) may re-stimulate such feelings and a phobia can result.

You may try to control these feelings, stifling the natural responses to survive by running away from the threat (or sometimes by behaving aggressively), but your brain still produces all the necessary survival changes in your body. Because you do not run away or fight, these feelings have to be suffered whilst stoically attempting to mask them from the eyes of others. This kind of experience often signals the commencement of a series of panic attacks, when the feelings can be so intense that the sufferers believe something really terrible is going to happen. They truly think that they are going to pass out, won't be able to breathe, or may even die. Were the victims able to recognize the panic attack for what it was – their survival kit doing a good job – they would be able to understand and accept that rapid breathing, an increased heart-beat, and sweating are all quite normal and necessary in a life-threatening situation. At that moment, if they could physically fight or run, the body's responses would be correctly utilized and they would feel fine again. However, logic does not co-operate with the irrational, emotional right half of the brain and it is extremely difficult – often impossible – for us to pause at such moments and calmly rationalize the situation. We do not stop to consider our responses when we feel threatened!

To avoid a repetition of the situation means avoiding those bad feelings, and so, in a way, the survival instinct achieves what it sets out to do. It prevents the person from going through that experience again. Refusing to shop, or not doing so alone, seems the only solution. However, going into a store is not, in reality, life-threatening, and avoiding doing so just becomes a wretched inconvenience.

The Way Out

You will recognize by now that such behaviour, however bizarre, has enabled you to survive. But behaviour patterns developed from childhood experiences, necessary then for your survival within that environment, are often no longer what you want or need in adult life.

You do know why you behave in the way you do, but have perhaps failed to recognize the causes or to relate them to your past. Often, they are so painful to recall that you may block them off and try to cope with life as if they never happened – and, for a while, this may work.

Some people manage to go right though life without ever dealing with past traumas or experiences that are spoiling or inhibiting their lives. It is not the way to get the best out of life, or to be completely free to develop as a mature human being, but they get by.

Taking your wonderful imagination, you can now go back and visualize scenes that have contributed to a present behaviour that you wish to change. Try and recognize where and how it started, and understand, without being critical, why you reacted in the way you did.

You can then use positive visualization to programme yourself to make those changes you want to make. By picturing yourself in control and using behaviour patterns that are going to get you the results you want, you strengthen positive feelings.

Please note! If you have a very traumatic history it is advisable to seek the help of a qualified therapist to help you undertake this 'going back'. Check first his or her qualifications first and make an initial appointment before commencing therapy. It is essential that you feel safe and can speak freely with your therapist.

The purpose of this book is to make you aware, to show you how you can help yourself, and to give you the techniques (mostly through visualization) that will equip you to deal with problems you may have or are likely to encounter.

Forgetting the Past

Some people ask me if I can help them to forget experiences. Of course I wouldn't dream of doing so. We learn from our experiences so that we know when *not* to do those things again. We especially learn from bad experiences. Should we forget those, we might do the same things and make the same mistakes all over again.

The important thing is to be able to let go of the emotional responses related to the bad or painful experience while retaining the benefits gained. In this way we hold on to the knowledge without the pain.

If a small child puts its fingers on the hot bar of an electric fire, it learns instantly not to do it again. Even before the child understands words, the mental images relating to that bad experience are stored in the Right Brain. When next the child comes near to such a fire, it will instinctively know not to touch. That is part of the survival process. If, however, every time the child sees an electric fire it goes into hysterics, this reaction in itself becomes a problem.

Remembering that emotions are not rational, such a child will go on using that same response into adulthood. The incident is not consciously recalled, but the adult simply states that he/she hates electric fires and may try to find all kinds of rational reasons for this feeling: they dry out the air, make it difficult to breathe, are expensive to run, or spoil the appearance of the room. A response which had been useful to the child's survival is no longer appropriate in adult life. It needs to be dealt with!

Here I am reminded of a young woman who came to me to give up smoking. While we were talking she asked me if, while dealing with the smoking, I could do something to prevent her being frightened when her boyfriend playfully put the pillow over her face. Imagine what might have happened if I had been able to do so?

When I ask you to picture areas of your past and to use various visualization techniques to 'undo' or to 'let go' of the bad experience, you will still be able to recall it consciously when you choose to do so – and if you choose not to, it doesn't matter. Your unconscious mind never forgets anything. It may not always be easy to transfer an experience to the Left Brain so that you can think about it in words, but it will remain safely stored away, becoming part of your survival kit.

Case History

Brenda is a middle-aged woman with a grown-up family. When she came to see me I learned that she had suffered all her life from a stutter. She had a lovely personality and many friends. The speech problem had not stopped her from getting on with life and she felt happy and fulfilled. 'The stutter,' she explained, 'is just a nuisance.'

As the speech problem had originated in her early childhood – she could never remember a time when she didn't have it – I used hypnosis to take her back to identify the start of the problem.

Brenda, at the age of four, had been adopted. The new, caring parents (for whom she felt much love and respect) had not only given her their surname, but also a new Christian name. From that moment she began to experience confusion. Whenever anyone asked her name she would hesitate – *Who was she now?* The hesitation became a stutter and overflowed into anything else she had to say.

During hypnosis, Brenda could clearly recall herself as that confused little girl of four. I asked her, as the caring mother that she now was, to take the little girl into her arms and reassure her.

Afterwards she told me that when she visualized doing this, the child somehow seemed to blend into her body, and it was a most wonderful feeling.

From then on Brenda's speech improved and she needed no further treatment. Such a positive outcome was also for me a wonderful and inspiring experience. It confirmed, once again, just how powerful visualization can be in effecting change.

Exercise 3 – Dealing with Past Negative Experiences

1 Gently close your eyes, relax and imagine yourself in a beautiful room that you have created. You had all the money you needed to make this room attractive, warm, and comfortable. There is an old, open fireplace with a crackling log fire in the hearth; some photographs or pictures hang on the walls and there is a bowl of flowers on a polished coffee table beside you – you notice the colour of the flowers and you may even be able to smell the faint perfume from them. You sit in a comfortable armchair in front of the fire and relax . . .

2 Pay attention now to the feelings and sensations in your body as you let go and relax. Check the feelings in your toes, your feet, your leg muscles as you let go and relax. Feel your stomach muscles relax . . . Notice

the rhythm of your breathing as you sink down deeper and deeper . . . Your breathing will have slowed and that's perfectly fine; the same thing happens each night as you go to sleep. You allow a calm peaceful expression to pass across your face as you relax all of the muscles in your scalp and forehead. You can feel your tongue resting comfortably inside your mouth as you let your jaw relax. Now let the muscles in your neck and shoulders relax. As you do so imagine all the stress and tension from your head, neck and shoulders flowing down your arms and out through the tips of your fingers. Notice the feelings in your hands as you relax deeper and deeper . . . Be aware of your own signals as you go to your own natural state of alpha level . . .

3 Consider a problem you have, or a behaviour pattern that bothers you – one that seems to have been with you for a long, long time . . . You would like to be able to do something about it and you need to know where it first started and what caused you to respond in that way.

4 As you continue to relax in your comfortable room, imagine putting on an video cassette of your past. You are holding the controls in your hand and you can run the video backwards or forwards as you wish. You watch the screen and, like a detective, you search for clues. Where did it all begin? You have no need to go back and *feel* again those feelings related to that time but only to *watch* from a distance. You are curious. When did your unwanted behaviour start? What caused it to happen?

5 Continue watching your past on the video film as you go back in time. Each picture that you recall will have some special significance for you. There is a valid reason why your mind has chosen this moment to

recall what you are viewing. The adult part of you may think some things you recall are insignificant, of little value, but when it happened you were much younger and would have felt quite differently about it.

6 When you feel that you have found the root of your problem, where it all started, stop the picture and look at it. Be curious, be inquisitive. See where your responses came from. Whatever your problem may be – take your time. This is an adventure. You are mature enough now to look at the past and to resolve past problems. Remember, you are only watching past events from a distance – *you do not get emotionally involved.* (Should memories become too painful, you have the controls in your hand and can simply switch off, open your eyes and wait until another time when you feel ready to try again.)

7 You are now able to recognize that what happened in the past belongs to the past and need have no influence on your present life or future. You no longer want or need those responses. You are ready to let go of those old emotions and behavioural patterns, and as you realize this the picture fades . . . Watch it getting fainter and fainter . . . It disappears completely . . . Now you take a deep deep breath and let go . . .

8 You remove the video cassette from the machine and drop it into the fire. Sitting back comfortably in your chair, you watch it safely and immediately shrink and melt away . . .

9 Picture yourself now set free from those old feelings and responses. You are able to accomplish that which previously caused you problems . . . Enjoy the experience of your new freedom.

10 Count slowly backwards from five to one, open your

eyes and return to full conscious awareness, feeling relaxed, refreshed and at peace with yourself.

Note: As an alternative, you may find that visualizing a cord connecting you to the screen – symbolizing the ties to the past – and then cutting the cord and letting the picture fade from the screen completely, is a very effective way of dealing with old emotional ties.

5

Changing Beliefs – Achieving Goals

Change

It is impossible to avoid change. We are going to grow up, mature and become old whether we like the idea or not. For many people the thought of growing old is viewed with dread. It is rare to hear anyone say that they are looking forward to growing old. However, we often hear people say they are looking forward to retirement.

What is the difference? In the first instance there is no anticipation of anything good happening. In the second there is a positive anticipation of all the good things the retired person will have time to enjoy – travel, hobbies, visiting friends, staying in bed for an extra hour in the mornings.

Whether we view change with dread or anticipation depends entirely on our point of view. We are constantly experiencing change and it can bring great rewards. But if the thought of change holds fear, if it creates negative thoughts and feelings, we try to avoid it.

Change can be very frightening. Although the situation we are in may be one we would like to change, fear of the unknown may cause us to hold back. That which is familiar

We can easily and simply change the way we see ourselves.

gives a kind of security, even though it is often not what is really wanted.

By viewing change as something to look forward to – a desired goal – expectation is born. The thought of change begins to feel good.

The Belief System

As we grow and develop, things happen to support our belief system. If a child is constantly being let down or disappointed by its parents, it will eventually stop looking forward to anything new or good happening. It thus becomes better *not* to look forward than to experience disappointment, for disappointment is painful and must be avoided. A negative attitude towards life gradually develops.

When no one goes along with what you believe you eventually discard that belief as wrong or worthless. A child told often enough that he is shy, clumsy, stupid, and unable to do things for himself, grows up believing those things to be true and will look for evidence to support those beliefs.

Beliefs must be fed and nurtured. We often do this for ourselves to enable us to feel safe and secure: *I knew I was right not to trust him . . . I knew it would happen . . . I knew I would never be able to stick to a diet . . . I knew I couldn't stop smoking for more than a week.* See what is happening? Tell yourself something often enough and you end up believing it.

Changing Beliefs

How do we set about making changes that we truly desire?

Take a little time and think about something that you wish to change. Ask yourself how it will affect you and your family. Spend time really picturing those changes. See them from both points of view – all the good things that can happen as a result of this change, and the negative effects.

You decide you still want to go ahead. Maybe you have no choice. Once the decision is made, focus on all the positive things this change will bring about. It will help your motivation to see these things as beneficial to you, improving the quality of your life.

Moving house is a change that affects most of us at some time in our life. Focusing on all the familiar things you are going to miss will make moving a very miserable affair and you may never settle in your new home. Looking forward to creating a new garden, making new friends, inviting old ones to visit, exploring untried restaurants and new places, can completely change the way you feel about your new home.

I remember feeling quite devastated when one of my sons informed me that he and his wife were moving to

Canada and intended to put down roots there. At first I was overwhelmed by a sense of loss. I imagined that I would hardly ever see my little grandson and that he might even forget who I was. I knew I would miss them popping in unexpectedly to see me. They would be absent from family parties . . . and so it went on.

Then I began to think about my visits to them. I thought of the gifts I would take to surprise them, and all the news we would have to exchange. I imagined their pleasure in showing me their new country. I also began to plan the things I would do when they came home to visit. Suddenly I realized that in two weeks each year we would possibly do more talking, and spend more concentrated time together than we had done during a whole year when they lived in England. And then there were all the phone calls to look forward to . . . The situation hadn't changed – but my viewpoint had!

All it takes to make change is a positive viewpoint. From time to time this needs to be strengthened and enhanced by using visualization. Eventually you will find it hard to remember why you ever resisted that change or experienced any doubt.

Achieving Goals

To achieve your goals it is necessary for certain things to happen.

1 **Expect to succeed**. The powerful effect of expectation should never be underestimated – it almost seems to *make* things happen. Expectation has a tremendous influence on us and those whose lives touch ours. Without any expectation of the desired goal being achieved, the thought becomes an unfulfilled daydream, a kind of hopeless wishful thinking.

 A hobby of mine is painting and some people who

view my pictures remark, *I could never do anything like that!* When I ask how long they have been trying, the response is almost always the same: *I only did art at school – I was never any good at it.* To this I reply by telling them that neither was I, but that I have been practising for forty years, and after forty years of doing something I would expect to be at least competent. Because these people have no expectation of being able to paint they never even get started.

Expectation is the first required ingredient if you are to achieve your goal, and remember that little comes to us without some effort or dedication on our part. Stopping smoking or losing weight requires both involvement and determination to achieve your goal. No hypnotherapist can stop you smoking or help you lose weight unless *you* decide to do so.

2 **Believe in yourself**. How can you ever expect others to have confidence or belief in you if you yourself nurture doubts?

3 **Be patient with yourself**. Give yourself time. You don't have to learn quickly or achieve overnight success – you will get there in your own way and in your own time. Some people have taken a university degree in their 80s.

4 **Never lose sight of your goal**. Use the end result to motivate you – see it as the fulfilment of your desires.

5 **Use your imagination**. Whenever you think about your goal, picture yourself succeeding. The pictures in your mind are what rules your world. If you cannot picture yourself 'doing', you cannot 'do'.

You may need to start in a small way, but a tiny seed can grow into an enormous tree.

If painting is something you would like to do, perhaps the way to start is with a pencil and paper. Simply sketch the things around you. Attempting something too ambitious can put you off for life.

To lose weight you could begin by cutting out sweets and chocolates – but don't forget the exercise! This helps to improve the metabolic rate and you start burning off those unwanted calories. There are hundreds of books on the market all claiming to have the answer to those excess pounds; if even one had the answer the rest would disappear from the shelves. *You* know why you are overweight – once you acknowledge this you can use self-hypnosis and visualization to strengthen your resolve to do something about it.

If you want to stop smoking, try reducing the amount you smoke by 10 per cent each week if giving up completely seems too drastic a step.

Whatever you decide to do – KEEP IT UP! Focus frequently on all the benefits your goal will bring.

Where your problem is a long-standing one, such as excess weight, you will find it best to go first to alpha level and to identify the cause. Often, overeating (the only real cause of being overweight, excepting fluid retention) may be fulfilling a leftover desire from childhood to please mother. There may be a sense of guilt at wasting food. It can be a substitute for love, success or recognition. Being overweight is often a cry for help.

It helps sometimes to replace a bad habit with a more positive habit. For example, taking exercise, instead of sitting eating a box of chocolates in front of the television, will help you control your eating habits; drinking a glass of water or chewing on a crisp raw carrot can satisfactorily replace that peanut butter sandwich.

You can use Exercise 3 to go back and identify the root of your problem, acknowledge the cause, and then deal with it.

Alternatively, 'Talking to Your Unconscious Mind', detailed in Exercise 6, will enable you to identify the reason why you smoke, overeat, bite your nails, etcetera.

Exercise 4 – Achieving Your Goal

1 Make yourself physically comfortable and relax. Close
   your eyes and picture yourself going down ten wide
   stone steps into a beautiful garden. Breathe deeply in
   and out and quietly count each step as you go down into
   the garden . . . At the foot of the steps pause and look
   around you. What season is it? It can be any time of the
   year you choose. Notice the flowers, the shrubs, the
   rustle of the leaves and the sound of birds chirping.
   Perhaps you can see butterflies or a fish pond . . . Take
   your time and create a garden you can enjoy. Wander
   through your garden and as you do so notice the texture
   of the path beneath your feet and feel the gentle warmth
   of the sun on your skin . . . Presently you will come upon
   a seat where you can sit down and relax even more.

2 You are relaxed and at alpha level. Now consider a goal
   you want to achieve. Ask yourself, *When I reach my goal,
   how will this change my life? How will it affect others? Do I
   truly want this?* Having confirmed that this goal is something you really desire, repeat the following.

   I am determined to . . . .
   I can . . . .
   I will . . . .
   You may then add something like:
   When I have . . . .
   I will be able to . . . .
   When I no longer . . . .
   I will be able to . . . .
   (Where I have left dots, use your own words to state
   your goal.)

3 Picture yourself leaving your seat and continuing
   through the garden. You begin to create something

beautiful or useful – perhaps you feel like planting something, making a rockery, filling a pond or playing with a child . . . You may have to knock down an old wall before you can begin to create. (Whatever you are doing with the visual part of your mind will have a corresponding positive effect on your unconscious responses.)

4 Consider the benefits achieving your goal will bring: improved good health, confidence, a better standard of living, a sense of self-worth, self-esteem, recognition, friends, respect . . .

5 When you have completed this, count slowly backwards from five to one, gently open your eyes and return to full conscious awareness, feeling relaxed, refreshed and at peace with yourself.

Note: If all this seems too hard to begin with, start by choosing a simple goal, one that is easily within your reach, or one where you need only an extra little push to get you going: For example, rising promptly when the alarm goes, taking regular exercise, starting a new project in the house such as decorating a room, putting up shelves, cleaning out the attic.

As you begin to get results, your belief system will be strengthened. You will truly begin to feel that you can do anything you set out to do.

Repeat this exercise on a daily basis until you get the results you wish to achieve.

Pausing occasionally throughout the day and visualizing yourself achieving your goals is an excellent way to strengthen positive feelings.

6

Confidence and Self-Esteem

Confidence

Some people seem to be born with it – they appear to fear nothing. They are the people who are always ready to have a try, nothing seems to overwhelm them, failure doesn't bother them. If things go wrong for them in business, before you know what's happening, you hear that they have started another one.

What is it that makes some people so confident, so self-assured? How do they differ? Where did they learn to be so sure of themselves, so positive? Again we return to our formative years. This is usually where confidence, or the lack of it, is formed.

Success breeds success. When you are praised, made to feel good about your achievements, it spurs you on to attempt something more daring, more adventurous. You can see this very clearly demonstrated by watching any small child. Through no fault of our own, some of us are made to feel unsure, unworthy, a failure, or that we are different.

To be confident you need to feel sure of yourself. Possessing a good sense of self-worth results in a good strong ego. To have a good sense of self-esteem it is essential that you have a good opinion of yourself.

What causes us to have a poor opinion of ourselves and doubt in our own ability to succeed? There are two primary influencing factors: other people's opinion of us, and comparison with others.

What Other People Think of Us

We have an inborn need to be like others, to be accepted. This herding instinct enables us to feel safe.

At school, through teasing, we can be made to feel inadequate, inferior, different, unacceptable – and it can be very destructive. You are likely to be teased if you are too short, tall, fat, thin, wear glasses or a tooth brace, speak with a different accent – almost anything can become a point of ridicule and there doesn't seem much you can do about it.

Case History

A lady came to see me who felt everyone was looking at her. She was convinced that they saw her as hideous. It came out that as a small child in school she had been learning to knit when the teacher called her to the front of the class. She stood her on a desk and told her to show the rest of the children what she had been doing. Proudly the child complied. The teacher then pointed out that the way she let go of the needle each time she wound the wool around it was wrong. At that moment she felt she just wanted to die; her cheeks became rosy red and she burst into tears. At 53 she still carried the emotional scars from that experience. Her unconscious mind had decided in its own way that it was because of the way she *looked* that she was unacceptable to society.

By using visualization she was able to 'undo' the incident. Her immediate response was quite wonderful to witness.

Why do others try to belittle us? The answer is quite simply that by drawing attention away from themselves they feel safe. *They* have the problem and try to hide behind unkind remarks, the teasing and bullying. It is well known that all bullies are cowards at heart.

Confidence can also be learned or destroyed within the home environment. A shy, retiring parent can be the example from which a child learns. To give your children one of the greatest gifts in life, nurture confidence. At the very least, support them in every way so that they may experience and learn, assured of your support and certain of your love and approval.

Children thrive on praise but I have never known a child blossom under criticism. Where children feel they are gaining approval and experience praise, they will, without any persuasion from parents or teachers, actively want to go on and do more.

Of course I am not suggesting you never correct a child. It is often necessary to point out that things could be achieved more easily or successfully by doing them differently. But don't put a child down – especially not in front of others!

Remember the headmaster who was so confident in addressing a large crowd but could not get up on the dance floor? Most people have areas where they feel confident and others where they appear to fail miserably. Believing that we are doing things badly, or are being laughed at or criticized by others, can be a powerful deterrent.

The answer lies within the story of the schoolmaster. Once he had learned how to dance correctly, he felt confident in displaying his skills in front of others.

Everyone has had to learn how to do whatever it is they now appear to do better than you. Impatient drivers who honk their horn because the learner is taking a while to pull out from a junction or roundabout have forgotten that they were once struggling to learn the very same thing.

Some of us, through indoctrination or religion, have been brought up to believe it is a sin to demonstrate confidence and that being 'big-headed' should be strongly discouraged. In reality the 'big-heads' of this world are only shouting loudly to boost their own poor self-image. When you know you can do something well you have no need to keep telling people. A quietly confident person is, in reality, very attractive and good to have around.

Comparison With Others

Comparing ourselves with others can make us feel inadequate, and we feed this with negative thoughts such as: *I could never do that . . . I'm useless at everything . . . I know I'll fail . . . I'm bound to get it wrong.*

It is a peculiar quirk of human nature to focus on failure. We reinforce our failures by re-living them again and again until we are utterly convinced there is no way out, and we have truly dug a deep hole for ourselves.

By comparison with others we are made to feel inadequate.

The wonderful truth is that each of us is unique, and everyone has his or her own special contribution to make – skills such as being a good listener, understanding the elderly or having patience with a small child are just as important as being able to fly an aeroplane or write a technical journal.

How do we overcome a poor self-image? What are we actually battling with inside ourselves?

Once you realize that the real struggle is between you and the way you see yourself, you can begin to do something about it. To do this you focus on your good points, on the positive things about yourself.

Don't be put off by people who think they are better than you. They have their own problem. This is usually their own inflated opinion of themselves and often takes the form of snobbery. To think you are superior because you had the privilege of a better education or upbringing, totally negates that privilege. You have to earn the respect of others. Respect isn't an automatic right through birth or education, nor through having wealth.

As you focus on the things you do well and the things you have achieved, your opinion of yourself will begin to grow and your confidence and ability to increase. Strange little thoughts will begin to creep in: *Perhaps I will have a go . . . I might just make it . . . There's no harm in trying*.

Remember that being different doesn't make you better or worse – you are simply you, with your own unique qualities and your own individual contribution to make. No one else can feel as you do; no one else has your sense of humour or your way of seeing things; no one else can love as you do; no one else has the same fingerprints; no one else can even write your name exactly as you do.

Building Confidence

To begin the journey from seeing yourself negatively to seeing yourself positively, use visualization. Remember, you can't be good at anything without practice, and all things start in the mind. *The key to your success is your imagination.*

Ask yourself: *What would happen if I were confident?* Perhaps you are afraid of losing friends, of being seen as bossy or self-opinionated. Certainly some people may be surprised at the changes in you. But if they really care about you, they will be delighted for you with your new freedom. Be assured, *confidence sets you free*.

Some men unconsciously destroy the confidence of their partners because this makes them feel safe and gives them control. Once the wife/partner begins to show confidence they feel threatened. Often they have been conditioned into believing it is the male role to be authoritative. They think that they will lose respect should they allow their own vulnerability to be exposed.

The image of the dominant male is learned through his cultural background. It is very difficult for him to see that he can still have respect and love without continuing to exercise what he sees as his rights or duty.

For those women who find that they are being 'put down' in order to support the male image, there *is* something you can do. Having built your confidence (by using techniques given in this book), you can help your partner to build *his* self-image. He will then no longer feel threatened and his need to dominate will diminish. You can then live as equals, supporting and nurturing that which is best within each of you. This may sound difficult to accomplish if you have been in a submissive role for a long time, but it is possible. It is important to set out to improve what you have together and not to destroy your partner.

There are, of course, many examples where it is the woman who plays the dominant role but here again the behaviour is prompted by fear. Being in control seems the only way in which such women can safely function.

There are men and women who will deliberately belittle their partner in front of others, taking every opportunity to show him/her in a bad light. This behaviour is often prompted by fear, a misguided set of values, a need to be noticed. This again is a case where the inner self is in need of attention. When you feel good about yourself you have no need to diminish others.

Some people fear that if they appear confident and/or capable, others will take advantage of them. The truth is that confident people are not afraid to say 'no'. They do not suffer the anxiety of appearing rude, nor do they fear rejection or worry about being seen in a 'bad light'. When they decide to refuse they reply firmly: 'Just now it is not possible – or convenient.' In life, however, we observe that confident people do seem to cope with far more than those who are trapped by their own inadequacies.

At first, if you find it difficult to picture yourself doing something with confidence, create a picture of someone you know who demonstrates the kind of confidence you would like to possess. Imagine him or her doing something you would like to be able to do. How do they approach it? What body posture do they use? What expression do you see on their face? How do you think they are feeling at that moment?

Now imagine that you could slip inside their skin and experience doing that thing the way they do . . . How does it feel? After a while step outside, and with that new knowledge see yourself approaching the same task, challenge or goal. Notice how different you now feel. Why choose to feel bad about something when you can choose to feel good about it? You can do it!

The first step towards confidence is to realize that we

are all equal. Of course you are going to meet people in life who can do things that you can't do – most of us can't walk a tightrope or fly an aeroplane, some of us aren't very good at singing or baking a cake – but there will be things that you can do that others cannot. This doesn't make us better or worse, and certainly the world needs people with different attributes and skills.

How dull life would be if one was born with the ability to do everything without struggle, endeavour or dedication. There would be no challenges, no sense of achievement, no thrills, no excitement. If everything was always available to us at any time, life would hardly seem worth living – and what boring creatures we would be!

Here I would like to share with you a lovely little story about Jean-Paul. At the age of four he moved from Montreal to England. Until that time he had spoken only French. Reaching his fifth birthday meant starting school and learning in a new environment that was totally English. He is a very adaptable little boy, and after one term could communicate well in his second language.

However, after a year his parents decided to return to Montreal and he was transferred to a school where French once more prevailed. This switching schools and languages slowed his reading in French. One day in class, while reading aloud, he found himself being laughed at by the other children as he floundered over some of the words. Abandoning his book, he turned to the class: 'So what!' he said. 'Maybe I can't read as well as you, but I can speak two languages and you can't.' Here is a young man who is never going to let anyone dent *his* confidence.

Assertiveness

To succeed in life, to get things done, to prevent people walking all over us, it is sometimes necessary to be assertive.

It sounds simple, but we all know it isn't. We worry about creating the wrong impression, we don't like to make a nuisance of ourselves, we become anxious over the possibility of a confrontation or aggression – it doesn't seem worth all the fuss and it is undoubtedly easier to do nothing.

There is nothing wrong in being assertive so long as it is done courteously – and yet we avoid it. It is often seen as a last resort.

The way to be assertive is to build your sense of ego. When you feel sure of yourself the doubts melt away. While this is happening (and by using self-hypnosis you will succeed), here is a way that has helped me to be assertive in everyday situations.

Ask yourself, if you were in the position of the other person or persons, would you want someone to tell you? If you had sold inferior goods, would you rather the customer brought them back or lose that customer? – or worse still, have them go around telling the story to others! If something you had said (or done) was causing anger or hurt, would you not want that person to tell you so that the situation could be resolved? When you look at things from the other point of view, being assertive is often better than saying nothing.

Thoughts such as: *Will they believe me? Am I really justified in making this complaint? They won't like me after I've told them. Someone's going to get embarrassed*, come about when you focus on the negative aspects of being assertive. Seeing it as a positive step will help you to present your case in the best possible way.

Exercise 5 – Building Your Confidence

1 Make yourself comfortable and relax. Look across the room and focus your eyes on something in front of you. Anything will do – a picture, a mark on the wall, a lamp ... As you continue to focus on that spot, begin counting slowly backwards from 500 quietly to yourself . . . Continue counting until you feel your eyes getting tired and wanting to close. As soon as they feel ready to close, let them go. Don't struggle to keep them open; they will naturally begin to feel tired or watery and start to blink. Let everything happen naturally.

2 When your eyes have closed, stop counting and mentally check that each part of your body is completely relaxed. Feel your toes relax, your legs, your body ... Allow a calm, peaceful expression to pass across your face; let your mouth and lips relax. Imagine all the stress and tension from your head, neck and shoulders flow down your arms and out through the tips of your fingers ... Be comfortably aware of the feelings and sensations in your body as you relax to alpha level.

3 Choose something you would like to be able to do, if only you had the confidence – something that until now you have felt was out of reach. Don't make it impossible to attain – you may have missed the opportunity of playing for England but there are plenty of other things to choose from. Make sure that it is something you *really want to happen* . . .

4 Place that on one side for a moment and think now of something that you do really well. Something you know you do at least as well, if not better, than other people: cleaning a car, writing a letter, baking a cake, gardening, ironing a shirt. A sense of accomplishment is what you

are seeking, feeling pleased with yourself when the task is completed. Imagine doing that task now and notice exactly how you are feeling as you do it ... Perhaps you are so relaxed you hardly have to think about it. You are stress free, certain that it will come out right. Visually complete the task. Experience that good feeling of having accomplished it ...

5 Now, taking your new goal, picture yourself doing it in that same manner – easily, successfully. Using the same expression, the same easy, relaxed attitude, the same calm assurance, picture it now ...

6 Say quietly to yourself: This is how I am going to ... *I can do it. I am confident. I will succeed.* (Take your time. Enjoy the sense of achievement.)

7 Count slowly backwards from five to one, open your eyes and return to full conscious awareness with a wonderful feeling of confidence in your own ability to do anything you set out to do.

Note: Repeat this exercise daily until you get the results you wish to achieve. Remind yourself often of your achievements and your goals. Enhance them with your imagination.

You will hear of people who endeavour to do things that have never been done before, and they succeed. They are the pioneers of this world, with courage and vision to take on the unknown. Without them human beings would never have reached the peak of Everest, sailed around the world, or sent a rocket to the moon. However, for the moment, let us settle for that which we know is possible – you can attempt the unknown when you've learned all you can from this book, thrown it on the fire or, hopefully, handed it on to someone else.

7

Stress Management

Identifying Stress

How do we know when we are stressed? Being in a state of stress can become such a habit that we are no longer aware that we are doing anything more than experiencing life as others do.

Some stress is necessary, for without it we would not be motivated to make change or progress. Stress can be the spur that helps us win or to achieve; it can motivate us to delegate, to find a better way of doing things. Stress can give us 'the edge' in a survival situation. In certain circumstances, being too 'laid back' means we are not prepared.

Unnecessary Stress

This is the kind of stress we are going to consider for we would do well to eliminate it totally from our lives. While it achieves nothing, it depletes our energy, affects our immune system, and spoils our quality of life.

Key Areas

Working with people from all walks of life, I have become aware that stress usually falls into one or more of the following categories:

- *Relationships* – with one's partner, parents, children, friends, colleagues, neighbours – even pets.

- *Health Fears*– real or imagined.

- *Confidence* – in doing almost anything, in dealing with others, in attempting anything new or different.

- *Location* – the place where one lives or works, especially if it involves making long journeys.

- *Change* – of any kind.

- *Work* – lack of communication, physical or mental inability to cope, difficult customers or colleagues, work overload, feeling unfulfilled; simply not liking what one is doing.

- *Money*– usually insufficient, causing fear and insecurity – but sometimes too much can also create stress.

Why Be Stressed?

All stress is self-induced. We may think others cause it, that we have no choice, but the reality is that we *do* have a choice. Once we are aware of this, we can choose whether to be stressed or not.

If this seems harsh, pause and think of someone you know who does a job that you consider would be stressful, and yet they seem to sail through it. Do they seem stressed? Do they enjoy their work? Would they change their job if they could? Absence of stress usually means that the job can be enjoyed and can result in a sense of fulfilment.

The secret is in the way you view the situation. For example, two nurses on a ward are doing exactly the same job. The ward supervisor/sister (who is suffering from corns on her feet and feeling thoroughly fed up) approaches the first nurse and proceeds to give her a severe telling-off. Watching the sister walk away the nurse is feeling close to tears. She wonders what on earth she has done to cause the tirade. The sister then approaches the second nurse and says exactly the same things. But as she walks away the second nurse grins wryly and wonders, 'What's up with her today?' In the same situation, depending on how they view it, one becomes very upset and the other remains calm and in control.

Stress Can Make You Feel Safe

Stress may have become so much a way of life that letting go can present a frightening picture. To a habitually

We can choose whether to be stressed or not.

stressed person, the very thought of letting go can make them feel as if they are 'falling apart'.

Think for a moment of a situation where you are aware of being stressed. This could be when you find yourself driving in crowded conditions, awaiting an interview with a difficult boss, or when you are expected to do two or more things at the same time. Finding yourself late for an appointment can send the heart-beat soaring. Think about a situation where you are stressed and really imagine the resultant feelings . . .

Now ask yourself: *What does it achieve? Could I function more efficiently, could I improve on the job, could I relate better to other people if I were not stressed in that situation?*

The chances are that as you visualize yourself without stress it will seem strange at first. But as you continue to enhance the picture in your mind, not only will it begin to look more attractive, but you will also notice that you actually feel physically more relaxed.

Nothing good can come from being stressed. However, I can promise you that every area of your life will be improved when you learn to cope in a relaxed manner.

Not being stressed will mean that you will feel free, have more energy, feel more motivated, have more time, feel fitter – and you will *most definitely* feel happier.

Recognizing Stress

How do you know when you are stressed? If it is a constant state how *do* you know?

Stress is the opposite of being relaxed. You cannot be stressed and relaxed at the same time – it is physically and mentally impossible.

As with all other things in our world, stress follows the law of 'cause and effect': something must happen to bring about this result.

Areas Which Cause Stress

Pressures from outside

- someone at work
- work overload
- someone close to you in your personal life
- neighbours
- debts you can't meet

Pressures from inside

- health problems
- concern about letting people down
- worry about what other people think of you
- lack of confidence
- imagined fears
- frustration
- your attitude towards life

These are some of the things that result in us feeling pressurized, and to which we often respond by feeling stressed.

Note: Guilt and bereavement can also be responsible for much stress – they are dealt with separately in Chapter 9.

Now ask yourself: *Am I Stressed?*

If you answer 'yes' to one or more of the following questions, then the chances are that you are suffering from stress.

- do you have difficulty sleeping?
- are you eating or drinking to excess?

- do you need drugs to help you cope with life?

- are you touchy or irritable?

- do you get anxious about things you used to take in your stride?

- do you often get 'flu or colds?

- have you a skin disorder?

- do you lack energy or enthusiasm for things you used to enjoy?

- do you get depressed?

- do you seem to have lost your sense of humour?

- is everything just too much bother?

What Can You Do About It?

1 Acknowledge that you are stressed. Hiding it to protect others or your own self-image only adds another burden.

2 Identify specifically what is causing you stress. Often you may know what this is but have failed to admit it. Making a list of everything that bothers you will help you to recognize the underlying cause. Talking things over with someone you trust is often all that is needed. One way of identifying the root of stress is to use the 'Talking to Your Unconscious Mind' technique given at the end of this chapter.

3 Decide now to make whatever changes are necessary to reduce or eliminate stress. If you truly believe you can't avoid or change the situation, the only thing left for you to do is to CHANGE YOUR VIEWPOINT OF IT. You will continue to do your best, but you *will not*, under

any circumstances, allow yourself, or anyone else, to put excess pressure on you. Learning to say 'no' sometimes is far easier than living with a stomach ulcer!

A sense of humour goes a long way towards relieving a stressful situation. Seeing the funny side of things can often help more than a handful of tranquillizers.

Frustration and anger can build up inside us when we are stressed until we feel ready to explode. By doing some activity, the energy is released and almost immediately we begin to feel better. (It's why some people kick the door or throw something.) Try to start a new hobby that you can use to dissipate this kind of energy – or try sawing logs, cleaning the windows, even a jigsaw puzzle kept handy on a tray will help.

It is a good piece of advice to remind yourself from time to time that you are only human, and that we all make mistakes sometimes. Don't be too hard on yourself – being cross, 'blowing your top' or feeling sorry for yourself occasionally is okay. There is nothing wrong with having high expectations of yourself, but impossible ones will destroy your confidence, diminish your self-image and may, eventually, prevent you from ever attempting anything new or challenging.

Recognize that it is possible to be deeply concerned without becoming stressed; caring and doing something constructive about a situation is far better than becoming so stressed that you are debilitated by those feelings. Some people confuse being stressed with caring – they think that if they don't feel very upset or stressed about something it may look as if they don't care. This isn't the best way of offering support or assistance.

Sometimes a situation becomes intolerable and there seems no escape. With no place to turn, the person involved believes they are left with only two alternatives: suicide or a 'break down'. I sincerely hope that this may never happen to you. But should things get that bad, there is another way out – you walk away. Sadly, by the time a hopelessly stressed person reaches this point, they are usually beyond being able to see any way out. No relationship, job, financial situation, or duty, is such that you have to die in order to escape it.

A great deal of research and work has gone into understanding and helping people who become 'trapped' in such situations. There are groups and organizations with trained people available where you can get the help and support you need. If your doctor seems not to understand your problem ask him/her to put you in touch with someone who is experienced and has time to listen. Sometimes this may mean finding a 'sitter' to give you a break from a caring role; you may need professional financial advice; you may need time away from your children; you may need help from a sex therapist. These people are available – ask for them.

The unconscious alternative, a 'break down', means that someone else makes the decision for you and you are removed from the situation which has become intolerable. Once recovered, the person often returns to the very same stressful situation, where nothing has changed. Within six months to a year they are back in a psychiatric ward wondering how it happened again.

Stress Can Kill

The medical world now acknowledges that stress contributes, in one way or another, to almost all known illnesses. When we are not stressed our body is in harmony; the necessary ingredients for our good health are readily available, and when we come into contact with germs or viruses our body's defence mechanism can immediately go to work.

Many apparently straightforward accidents are caused by stress. The mind and body cannot react quickly if they are in a constant state of stress.

Mental stress is a kind of distraction that prevents concentration. We are more likely to make errors of judgement when we are stressed.

A physiotherapist, questioning patients suffering from pain in the lower back, discovered that 80 per cent of them were trapped in a stressful situation at work, from which they could see no way out. By teaching them simple relaxation exercises, he noted that there was a marked improvement in their health and the problem tended not to recur.

Other Causes of Stress

Not all stress is caused by the way in which we see things or deal with them. It is now recognized that pollution, the food we eat, the effects of certain weather and lack of sunlight can all cause people to become stressed.

I wish there was a magic ingredient to counteract all these elements, but none has been found. The best way of protecting yourself is to eat as healthily as possible, take the amount of exercise and rest that your body needs, use relaxation exercises as described in this book, and deal with any cause of stress as soon as you become aware of it. In this way you will be giving your body the best chance possible to counteract outside alien conditions.

Organic Dysfunction of the Brain (ODB)

This problem has been researched over the past 20 years and is now acknowledged as the invisible cause of an enormous amount of stress in some people.

In some children, the natural reflex actions of the body do not develop normally as they grow, and because of this, any task requiring concentrated co-ordination, such as threading a needle, creates an excessive amount of stress. ODB sufferers are always stressed, and it takes only a little extra to push them 'over the top'. They can then become very angry, frustrated, desperate or depressed.

We can see this in young children of similar ages trying to put together a puzzle. One child will complete the task in minutes while another, after struggling for some time, may become so frustrated that the puzzle pieces end up being thrown across the room. This doesn't mean this child is excessively impatient or bad tempered but, rather, indicates that he/she needs extra care and understanding.

ODB is reversible. It takes about two years of exercises and should be done under the guidance of someone who specializes in dealing with this dysfunction.

Dealing With Stress

Once we have decided that stress isn't doing us any good and that life would be more pleasant and productive without it, we need to deal with it – by using visualization.

Below are two techniques which I find work well. You can try whichever one appeals to you, or use them at different times in different situations.

Exercise 6 – Talking to Your Unconscious Mind

1 Make yourself comfortable, relax, look across the room and focus your eyes on a spot in front of you: anything will do – part of a picture, a mark on the wall, a lamp ... As you continue to focus on that spot, begin counting

slowly backwards from 500 quietly to yourself . . .
Continue counting until you feel your eyes getting tired
and wanting to close. As soon as they feel ready to close,
let them go. Don't struggle to keep them open, they will
naturally begin to feel tired or watery and start to blink.
Let everything happen naturally.

2 When your eyes have closed, stop counting and mentally check that each part of your body is completely
relaxed. Feel your toes relax, your legs, your body.
Allow a calm peaceful expression to pass across your
face; let your mouth and lips relax. Imagine all the stress
and tension from your head, neck and shoulders flowing
down your arms and out through the tips of your fingers
as you let go and relax. Be comfortably aware of the
feelings and sensations in your body as you relax to
alpha level.

3 Imagine yourself in your own home. You are sitting in
a comfortable armchair or lying on your bed. Picture
your surroundings. Notice the position of the window
and door in relation to where you are? What colour
are the walls? What covers the floor? Can you see
pictures or photographs? Is there something in the room
that has a special meaning for you?

As you sit there relaxing and feeling safe and secure,
imagine that you can call before you your *unconscious
mind* – that part of you responsible for your emotions,
your dreams, your visual memories. Give your unconscious mind a shape, the first one that comes to you . . .
Now give it colour. The first colour you think of is fine.
Hold on to that image in your mind – it represents for
you your unconscious mind. In a few moments you are
going to ask it some questions and the very first thought
that comes back to you is the answer you need. Don't
consciously consider the answer – that's the Left Brain
trying to take over – just let the thought come . . . Now

quietly ask your image: Why am I stressed? . . . Whatever the answer, acknowledge it, don't deny it. This may be very different from the one you would have consciously given. Then say to your image: *I no longer want to respond to this situation/person by being stressed.*

Pause . . . allow your unconscious mind to accept this decision. Then say to your image: *Show me a better way of dealing with this problem so that I am no longer stressed by it.* Pause . . . relax . . . and wait for the answer. This may come in a single word, in a thought, or a mental picture.

Still keeping the image of your unconscious mind before you, ask it to take responsibility for making whatever changes are necessary. Say quietly: *Please take responsibility for making those changes that are necessary for my peace of mind and well-being.* (Perhaps your unconscious mind has chosen for you to be more assertive, or to give yourself more time; it may be that you need to communicate your feelings to others.)

4 Whatever change or changes you have chosen, picture yourself using that changed behaviour. If you feel less stressed or anxious when you view yourself using these changes, you will know they are right for you. Where you still feel some anxiety, this may be because it feels strange or different. In this case try the change, or changes, over the next few days. You can always do this exercise again and ask your unconscious mind to choose new options.

5 Thank your unconscious mind for co-operating in this wonderful way. Mentally drift, allowing whatever changes that have to be made internally to take place.

6 Count slowly backwards from five to one and as you do so, slowly open your eyes and return to full conscious awareness feeling confident and assured.

Note: Sometimes we do not seem to get an immediate answer when doing this exercise. This usually means that whatever changes are taking place are happening at a totally unconscious level. Maybe the Right Brain recognizes that the Left Brain would interfere if it knew. This is likely to happen if you are a very Left-Brain-orientated person and try to override the unconscious responses with logic. The wonderful thing is that, even so, you will still respond. After a while you will begin to notice that in certain ways you are behaving differently, that you have changed and that you are feeling good.

Repeat the above exercise whenever you feel there is a need.

Exercise 7 – An Alternative Way of Dealing With Stress

1 Make yourself physically comfortable and relax. Close your eyes and picture yourself going down ten wide stone steps into a beautiful garden. Breathe deeply in and out and count quietly to yourself as you go down each step. At the foot of the steps, pause and look around you. What season is it? Notice the flowers, the shrubs, the sounds of birds. Perhaps you can see butterflies or a fish pond . . . Take your time to create a garden you can enjoy. Wander through your garden and as you do so, notice the texture of the path beneath your feet and feel the gentle warmth of the sun on your skin . . .

2 Presently you come to a beautifully mown green lawn. As you walk across it you see in front of you an old well surrounded by a low stone wall with a little thatched roof over the top of it. As you get closer you see that there is a carved wooden box, like an old-fashioned casket, lying on the wall. It has an open lid fixed with

brass hinges, and a catch at the front of it; lying beside it is an open padlock. When you reach the well you pause and, taking the box in your hands, you put into it all the things you recognize that are causing you to be stressed. Name them to yourself as you put them into the box . . . Take all the time that you need to do this. When you have finished, close the lid, fix the padlock round the catch and drop the box into the bottomless well. Let go . . . let go completely. Let go of fear, let go of guilt, let go of pain, let go of a sense of failure, let go of personal hurt feelings . . . Now take a deep, deep breath and relax.

3 You walk on until you find a place where you can sit down and relax in the sunshine. Stay there for a while and enjoy the sense of peace and tranquillity flowing through you. Give this feeling a word – one that will have a special meaning for you – and as you say the word quietly to yourself, clasp your hands together for a moment . . . Hold on to that good feeling. From now on, whenever you feel unwanted tension or stress building up, you have only to pause, breathe deeply, clasp your hands together in exactly this way and say your 'cue word'. Separate your hands again and as you do so you will relax and be able to proceed calmly and confidently. (By doing this you have created your own anchor.)

4 Count slowly backwards from five to one, open your eyes and return to full conscious awareness, feeling confident in your own ability to cope with life in the way you choose.

Note: While running a course on using the unconscious mind, I used this visualization with a group of adult students. One woman admitted afterwards that this had made her feel very guilty – she had found herself trying to stuff her mother down the well! I suggested that if she put down the well only those things about her mother that she found stressful, it would allow her to focus on her good qualities.

After doing this, to her surprise, she realized that there were indeed things about her mother that she liked and could enjoy. Until she used visualization in this way they had been completely obliterated by the negative feelings. After these visualization exercises she felt convinced that those things she had found irksome or distressing would no longer bother her. What she had done was to change her focus from the negatives to the positives – which is what all good relationships are based on. (More of this in the next chapter).

Forming Your Own Protection

There is a way of protecting yourself from stress and pressure that I find very effective. It takes only a few moments and once programmed is readily available whenever you need it.

Take a few moments to relax. Close your eyes and picture a protective screen surrounding you. This screen can take any form you like – I have had people visualize everything from aluminium foil to an electric field. The important thing is that you see it clearly while knowing it is invisible to everyone else.

From now on this is your protection from outside pressure or stress. No matter where it comes from, you have only to picture your screen preventing any stress from reaching you. You can even create a kind of cartoon in your mind and imagine everything bouncing off it. The more 'way out' or bizarre the images you choose, the easier it is to visualize and hold those pictures.

In pausing and using this visualization whenever you feel pressurized, you can actually help to change the way in which you respond. With practice, you will soon be able to picture this protection as easily as blinking when something comes too close to your eyes.

8

Relationships and Communication

Relationships

Unless you are a recluse, it is impossible to avoid relationships. We are involved in them constantly for they are the very structure on which we build our lives and our security.

The dictionary defines a relationship as *a link or connection – the state of being connected or related*. But it is *the way in which we connect* that is important to understanding and improving a relationship.

Our first relationship is normally with our mother. This usually feels good. We are nurtured, loved and comforted, and this experience forms the foundation for all future relationships – it sets the pattern. Gradually, as we develop, we form further relationships, including those with our father, brothers, sisters, grandparents and other close relatives. Within a few years we begin to venture outside the security of home, and relationships develop with friends, neighbours, teachers and people in authority. We expand our world.

Wherever there are needs which are satisfied, a relationship is formed. Even a man and his dog have a relationship where each fulfils the needs of the other: security, food and shelter are provided by the man, and the dog in return offers companionship, protection, a reason to take exercise. They exist peacefully together.

We also have a relationship with our environment and the world in which we live. Sadly, failing to recognize this has led to the devastation of forests, pollution, and a drain on the Earth's natural resources.

We all have needs, they are the very essence of our being. A newborn baby's needs are totally satisfied by its mother. In those early days the needs of the mother are met in her instinctual sense of fulfilment in caring for her child; they are both content and there is a good strong relationship. If, for some reason, the mother resents the child, or actively wishes she had not given birth, then this satisfying relationship will not exist. The effects would soon become evident in the behaviour of the child and insecurity, an inability to express its feelings, angry resentment, or an over-demanding personality may develop.

It sometimes happens that a mother and her child are separated during those vital early years, and the resulting sense of loss can have a lifelong effect upon the child. This experience can influence all its future relationships. These unfortunate people find it hard to trust and have a deep fear of separation of any kind. Their emotions are often suppressed or denied. The unloved child, deprived of its mother, may become very possessive or jealous of anyone or anything they see as a threat.

When we first fall in love there is always a wonderful relationship. We focus totally on all the positive attributes of the object of our love and completely fail to see any faults or weaknesses. If questioned, we would probably deny that there were any, and we would truly believe this to be so. 'Blinded by love' describes exactly what we are. However, with time – for it is impossible to stay at that euphoric level in a realistic world for ever – we begin to notice some of the 'not so attractive things' about our loved one. We come down off 'cloud nine' and return to reality and the limitations of being human.

That's fine if each of the people involved is moving and adjusting at the same pace. The problems start when one of the couple begins to find fault or to offer criticism whilst the other is still totally focused on all the positives. What is meant as a harmless comment – 'You really do tend to over-cook the vegetables' or 'Couldn't you clean the bath after you've used it?' – can result in deep and lasting hurt. When we are in love we are so painfully vulnerable.

Discussing this with a friend, he told me that in the early days of his marriage the feelings between him and his wife were so intense that she could not bear to give him anything she considered less than perfect. One day she gave him an apple she had bought in the market, but when he bit into it he found himself looking at a small grub. The wife was devastated by this and for hours afterwards was quite inconsolable – an incredible overreaction to something others would see as amusing or of no consequence.

What Constitutes a Good Relationship?

If we have powerful needs and those needs are met by our partner, we are going to have a good, strong, enduring relationship. If one partner is happy to give and the other content to be always on the receiving end, this still constitutes a good relationship for it satisfies their completely different needs. The essence of a good relationship is that our needs are fulfilled. When they are not, the relationship will, in time, break down. A couple may continue to live together, they may even think they still have a relationship, but the truth is that they have become two people living in the same house without any real communication.

In the Beginning

The natural way to commence a relationship is by focusing on all the good things. It seems so easy at first to love your child, husband, parents, friend, but for this state to continue and to develop into something lasting, it is essential to keep on communicating. You need to take the time and make the effort required to fulfil each other's needs.

Although marriage is one of the most important relationships we will ever enter into (it's planned to last a lifetime!), it is amazing how little thought or time people put into making it work. Taking someone for granted within a relationship can be one of the most destructive forces it will have to endure. If things begin to turn a little sour, ask yourself if it is because you are no longer focusing on all the positives.

Most of us are going to be involved in relationships within our working environment. Here the same principle applies. When the first flush of novelty is over you must continue to communicate. Take time to reassess the way you are looking at things. Problems or dissatisfaction may arise simply because you have begun to see things from a negative point of view.

Communication

Communication is essential in any relationship. We seem often to expect our partners to be clairvoyant, believing that in some mysterious way they should know how we feel without our ever having made ourselves clear.

This is a particularly common problem within the sexual part of a marriage/relationship. How the male is supposed to know what the female likes or dislikes, what arouses her or puts her off, without any signals or communication from her is a mystery. I am told by sex therapists who deal with these problems that failure to communicate is one of the most common reasons for things going wrong. It can, of course, happen the other way round, but more often than not in these circumstances, it is the woman who fails to communicate her needs and desires.

Many things are recognized unconsciously and work out well without having to be analysed or discussed. Here, we are looking at ways in which relationships can consciously, and with a little more knowledge, be improved and made to last.

For two people to communicate it is essential that one is in a receptive, listening mode while the other is in an outgoing mode. When both are attempting to project their thoughts and ideas onto the other at the same time, no real communication can take place. This can be noted in conversations when one person (in the outgoing mode) is speaking, while the other, instead of being in the receptive mode is just waiting to butt in. They are both focusing on their own ideas, thoughts and objectives, instead of *really* listening and 'taking in' what is being said. Often this is what happens in an argument, thus preventing any real communication from taking place.

'I am communicating!'

Understanding Your Needs

The first step towards communicating your own needs is to understand them. If you find this difficult – and many people do, for they often have no idea what their needs are or what they want from a relationship – begin by noticing those things that make you feel good about yourself. Look for those things that bring joy, a sense of freedom, things that are guiltless.

When you watch a film or read a book, what is there about it that you enjoy? Within your answer lies a clue to your own needs. If the gentle way he touches her, or the loving way in which she greets him when he returns from work evokes in you a response, then consider if there isn't that same need within yourself.

In your working environment you may encounter people who expect you to know what they want without ever having explained to you the exact requirements of the job. Make it clear that in order to do the job to the best of your ability, things must be properly explained and regularly reviewed. It is such a fundamental principle but so often missed: when people are happy in their work, output is increased.

A friend of mine once went to work for a very successful business man. 'He didn't,' she told me, 'even bother to say good morning, or how are you?' He considered such things banal and a waste of valuable time. To her, it was a way of communicating that their day had begun and that they could work amicably together. She didn't stay long in his office and he lost someone who was extremely good at her job.

If, in your work, you recognize that your needs are not being fulfilled, ask yourself why you feel this way. Is it because you are bored, fed-up, unhappy, neglected? Does the job lack challenge? Is there too little or too much responsibility? Once you have identified the problem, *do something about it.* It may involve making a fuss or collaring a busy boss, but the chances are that he/she would prefer to listen and try to do something to rectify the situation than lose a good member of staff.

The Invisible Clues

Apart from verbal communication, we use our senses in other ways to enable communication to take place. Although the majority of people use their verbal ability to express themselves, and move their hands to help demonstrate what they are trying to communicate, we all have a tendency to rely on one sense more than the others.

Some people will first of all *picture* a thing, whereas others would recall that same thing by remembering the *feel* of it. Water is a good example of this. When I asked a group of people to recall the sea, I discovered that about 60 per cent of them saw it, 30 per cent heard it, and the rest imagined that they were actually in it.

For some people the smell or sounds connected with an experience help them to remember and to re-enter that memory. To understand how this works within yourself, it helps to be attentive to the way in which you specifically respond to things.

If we fail to recognize the way in which others access an experience, much is lost and many misunderstandings can result. To demonstrate how understanding this can save a relationship, let us look at the following example.

Case History
A young couple came to see me because their marriage was not going well. The problem lay with their sexual relationship. The wife, while assuring her partner that she still loved him, was no longer interested in sex. As a result of this the husband was feeling angry and

rejected. 'There's nothing wrong with me,' he protested. 'I can still perform all right. She's the one that's changed.'

While encouraging them to express their feelings, I watched the directions in which their eyes moved as they spoke.

I then asked a few questions and discovered something very interesting. Where he tended to access his initial sexual stimulation through touch and taste, the wife experienced hers through sight and sound. So what was wrong with that? Well, they made love in the dark and he didn't speak whilst this was happening. Unwittingly, he was denying her the two natural ways which would have led into the full experience of sexual fulfilment (which ultimately becomes a physical one). She could have enhanced her feelings by using her imagination if she had been aware of her problem, but she had no idea what was wrong.

They agreed to leave a soft light on when they made love. She could then see the expression on his face (this helped her emotionally) and he could see her body (this stimulated her sexually). He learned to talk a little when they were making love and their whole relationship improved. No one had been right or wrong. It wasn't anyone's fault. They had simply never discovered that they experienced things differently.

The direction in which people move their eyes when they are experiencing something or recalling a memory can differ, so a number of questions and noted responses are necessary to help you discover how you use your eyes in such a situation.

With a friend or partner, sit facing each other. On a pad draw a face. Put arrows as shown in the diagram.

Ask your partner the following questions and as you do so watch the direction in which his/her eyes move. After each set of questions mark this on your diagram. When

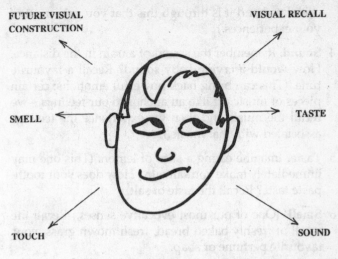

FUTURE VISUAL
CONSTRUCTION

VISUAL RECALL

SMELL

TASTE

TOUCH

SOUND

Getting to know how you experience things.

you have completed the list, change over and let your partner record your responses in the same way.

1 **Visual Recall.** What is the colour order of the traffic lights? Picture the clothes you wore last Sunday. What do you first see when you open your front door?

2 **Future Visual Construction.** Imagine a room in your house completely redecorated and with new furniture. Picture the order of the traffic lights using blue, pink and white instead of red, amber and green. Imagine how people would look covered with fur. (Picturing something that hasn't yet happened is something that inventors and creative people often need to do.)

3 **Touch.** Imagine how your hands would feel in very cold water? How it feels to sink into a comfortable armchair. How it feels to hold a small child's hand in yours? (If you find yourself picturing the event before being able to feel it, you will know that you are primarily visually

orientated and it is through this that you gain most of your experiences.)

4 **Sound.** Remember the sound of a train in the distance. How would a crying baby sound? Recall a favourite tune. (This can bring back powerful emotions; certain pieces of music act like an anchor to our feelings – we recall the music and then we experience the feelings associated with that music.)

5 **Taste.** Imagine eating a slice of lemon. (This one may immediately make you salivate.) How does your toothpaste taste? Recall the taste of salt.

6 **Smell.** (One of our most evocative senses.) Recall the smell of freshly baked bread, fresh mown grass, your favourite perfume or soap.

The eyes may appear to move in the same direction for more than one 'sense' – this is usually when your mind goes first to one experience and then over to another. For example, when asked to imagine freshly mown grass, you may first *picture* the lawn, or *hear* the mower before being able to recall the smell. In this case you would know that your sense of recall through smell is not very dominant.

If, sometimes, your eyes de-focus and stare ahead, there's nothing wrong with this, it is your way of helping you to recall or access certain experiences/memories. Nothing new has happened; it's simply that you have never noticed these things before.

Where you found it difficult to respond to some of the above questions, this usually indicates that those senses are not often called upon to help you access information. They can, however, be developed with practice.

Now, having some idea of which way your eyes move when you want to recall certain things, you can use this constructively to help you recall experiences, access information and develop some of your senses.

If you want to recall a tune and your eyes move up and to the left, turning your eyes in that direction should help you to remember it. In an examination, by moving your eyes in the direction of your 'visual recall', you can help yourself to recall certain information that you have previously seen written.

The reason all this works is that the eyes are attached to the brain – they have a working partnership.

Saving a Relationship

Relationships do break down, and sometimes there seems no alternative but to call it a day. If you feel a relationship is worth saving – and it will require effort from both parties – try to go back and see how things were in the beginning. Too many current negative thoughts can completely crowd out the positive memories.

I have listened to people declare they never really loved their wife/husband/partner and they can't imagine how they ever got together in the first place. Of course this just isn't true, but with so many bad thoughts and experiences to focus on, they have completely lost sight of anything good they ever had together.

By moving your eyes in the direction that helps you to recall past experiences you can enhance good memories by adding sound, touch and taste, where appropriate. These memories can then become so enjoyable that they completely blot out the bad, negative feelings. Imagine how lovely it would be to have all those good experiences available to you, and to be able to enjoy them again and again as if they happened only yesterday.

A second honeymoon, where you give your whole attention to each other, can help a floundering relationship. Taking time to discover what once made things between you so special may help get things back into perspective. It will enable you to see that all that is really needed is the determination to put each other first.

I realize this isn't going to be easy when children, family duties, the pressures of work, and meeting bills are all demanding your attention. But when the children have left home, what will you have? The answer should be, 'each other'.

An experienced maternity sister I knew, used to say to the young mothers in her care: 'Don't worry so much about the baby. It's the father you need to fuss over. He's going to be there long after that baby has grown up and left home.' And so he should be, if loving care and attention has gone into communicating and satisfying the needs of each other.

Case History
Penny had been suffering from a debilitating illness for a long time. During this period she had not had the mental or physical energy to attend to her marriage or even to consider how her husband was feeling. The marriage began to deteriorate until she wasn't sure she wanted to stay in it.

One day, she told me, she had imagined her husband dead and saw herself sitting on the edge of the bed looking at him. As she did so she realized that she was never going to be able to share anything with him again. This made her aware of how important he really was to her. She began to do those little thoughtful things that had been part of their relationship in the early days of their marriage – cooking his favourite meals, popping a note in his lunch box, buying him a small, unexpected present.

She was surprised and delighted with the response. The magic began to come back into their lives and they both realized they shared something very precious that they had almost lost.

Recognizing Change

One thing is for sure, we don't stay the same. The wife or husband who cries out in an argument, 'You aren't the person I married. You never used to be like this,' is attempting, unsuccessfully, to hold on to an impossible dream.

We do change and mature. The man or woman who still feels the need to behave like a teenager presents a pathetic figure. The needs of a 20-year-old are very different from those of someone in their 40s. Our needs are different again when we reach 60 and again at 70. We have to continually make adjustments. Most of the time this happens naturally, and with little or no conscious effort on our part.

Wanting to be constantly together when you first fall in love *is* natural, but it can become very stifling if this ultimately prevents either partner from pursuing his or her own hobbies and interests. To give up everything for each other is a programme for later discontent and recriminations.

It is also important to recognize that attempting to change people so that they fit into the mould we wish them to occupy, takes away their uniqueness and prevents honest communication.

Failing to recognize the changing needs in your children can result in frustration, tantrums, anger, resentment and guilt – and sometimes a total breakdown in the relationship. The very things from which you, at one time had to protect your child, become the very things he or she absolutely insists are essential to their happiness.

It is hard to hold back, to stop giving advice, and watch your child suffer from his/her mistakes. Taking the brunt of your child's anger and blame when, having held back in an attempt not to interfere, you are accused of not helping or caring, is another experience that so often goes with being a parent.

At times it feels that nothing you do is right and that the whole fabric on which you built your life as a parent is collapsing around you. This is a time when disillusionment and loss of confidence may threaten to engulf you.

However, rebellion, breaking away, becoming an independent human being, are all essential to a child's survival. You aren't always going to be around to protect and advise. What often seems like open defiance or rejection of your values or teaching, is an instinctual reaching out for the new in a changing world – a world in which they must one day survive without the support of parents.

Conversely, a child must also recognize that parents' needs change. Parents finally set free from responsibility may want to go off and 'do their own thing'. Always being there for the family to return home for Sunday lunch can become a burden. Grandparents may not always want to be available to have the grandchildren; there comes a time when, perhaps, they want a life without responsibility. Much as the grandchildren are loved, the grandparents may not feel able to cope with them for prolonged periods, or simply do not want to.

These are only a few examples and I am sure you can think of many more for yourself.

Rejection

With all the good will in the world, things don't always work out right between two people. Some people cannot remain faithful to one partner: they have a desperate need to keep making new conquests. It is as if they have frequently to prove to themselves that they are desirable. Others find that the person they trusted and believed was theirs for life, falls in love with someone else.

What do you do about it? After the initial hurt and anger there must be a time for assessing the situation. You need to ask, 'Do I love this person enough to work at trying to build a better, stronger relationship?' It has to be a two-way communication and cannot be achieved by yourself. Unless you can both view the relationship positively as something you want to try and put right, it cannot work.

Happily, more often than not, most couples want to give it another try. These are the sort of things that are said to me, and indicate hope: *If only my wife would give me more time . . . If only we did more together . . . I'm sure things would be better if we didn't always have to have her mother – then, yes, I would rather be married to her than anyone else.*

Take, for example, the case of Mike and Vikky, friends of mine whom I have known for more than 20 years. Their problem is that Vikky seems always to spoil any pleasure Mike has that excludes her. This has made him secretive. He feels the need to pretend not to find pleasure in things that he really enjoys in order to preserve that hobby or interest. At the same time, he told me, she is the only person he has ever met with whom he wants to live.

Vikky told me that she felt hurt and angry because Mike never seemed to give her any consideration when he wanted to do something. She felt he rejected her in preference for other things.

Here was a case where communication and understanding could improve a marriage they both really wanted to survive.

If, however, there is no real desire to rebuild and you see no alternative but to part company, hold on to the fact that feelings do diminish in time if you let them. By turning your attention to fresh interests and different challenges, a new life will emerge. This is particularly true of creative pursuits.

I'm sure you know of at least one person who has gone through a broken marriage or bereavement. They will have been hurt, and possibly felt devastated. At that time they believed they would never get over the loss. Then a year or two later you meet them and discover that they are very happily settled in a new relationship.

Every relationship is unique. It is wrong and does a new partner a great disservice to compare them with a previous one. Neither should we expect them to behave as did the first partner. They are individuals with their own unique contribution to make that has nothing to do with a past love.

Starting a Relationship

When running a seminar on relationships I have some-times been approached by people who tell me: 'My prob-lem is not how to improve a relationship, but how to get into one in the first place.'

What is it that prevents some men and women from ever finding a partner or close friend with whom they can share their lives, their hopes and dreams? The answer lies in their own concept of themselves. They can't believe anyone would want them as a friend, partner or lover. Their self-image is so poor that they convey this message without even speaking a word. Often the root of this problem is shyness.

If you have a longing to share your life with someone else, concentrate on building your confidence and self-esteem. If you don't like yourself, this is unconsciously conveyed to others. The message comes over loud and clear: *Why should he/she like me? I don't!*

I am sure you are not half as bad as you think. You have just been too busy focusing on negative thoughts about yourself to notice the good qualities you possess.

To meet and communicate with others is far easier if you pursue a hobby or interests that you can truly enjoy. By getting involved in things that matter to you, you will meet people with similar interests. It then follows quite naturally that you will be able to talk to them without the mental pressure of struggling to find something you think may hold their attention.

If you are interested in things, you become interesting. There is no need for pretence. People soon see through that anyway. If you talk with enthusiasm about that which interests you, it will draw others to you and the aura you create will be very attractive indeed.

Contrary to what many people think – quite illogically I may add – *we are not liked because of our looks*. People like us because of what we are: fun, friendly, gentle, kind, a good listener, trustworthy, courteous, caring – these are the qualities that attract friends. You don't need to be slim, beautiful, dressed in expensive clothes, clever or well-educated to be liked. You knew all that? Well, you would be surprised how many people truly believe beauty is essential to happiness.

The single most attractive quality in any human being is happiness. No matter whether it is a small child gurgling to itself in a pram, or an old person basking contentedly in the sunshine, they attract us. We want to move closer. In some inexplicable way we hope something of that happiness will brush off on us. It explains why people in love appear so attractive. Did you ever see an ugly bride?

Finally, and this is worth remembering, we do like people who make us feel good about ourselves. Looking outwards, setting about making other people feel comfortable and at ease not only takes the pressure off us but also makes us feel good.

Exercise 8 – Improving a Relationship

1 Close your eyes and imagine yourself sitting in a comfortable armchair . . . Before you is a child's blackboard

and easel. Several pieces of fresh white chalk are resting on a ledge at the front of the board. You lean forward and, taking a piece of chalk in your fingers, you write the first letter of the alphabet on the blackboard. When you have done this, say the name of that letter quietly to yourself, then erase the letter and proceed with the next one. Again look at it, say it quietly to yourself, erase it, and continue in this way through the alphabet until you reach the letter Z . . . As you erase this last letter, take a deep, deep breath, and as you breathe out, feel yourself drift down into your own natural state of alpha level. Notice your own physical signals as you let go and relax.

2 Imagine that you now stand up, leave your chair, and open the outside door. As you look out you see that it is a lovely evening and you feel a great longing to go out for a while. You put on comfortable outside shoes and a lightweight jacket . . . It is springtime and as you walk along you notice the fresh green leaves on the trees and you see the delicate yellow primroses in the hedgerow. Birds are chirping and there is the distant sound of an aeroplane. Presently you come to a beautiful woodland, safe and secure. You decide to take the path through the wood. It is so quiet and tranquil here, and as you walk along the woodland path the ground becomes soft under foot with years and years of fallen leaves and soft green moss. Sunlight is filtering through the leaves of the trees, coming down in shafts of light to touch the path before you . . . Soon you hear the sound of running water and see in front of you a lovely stream. You pause and watch the clear water sparkling as it ripples over the stones and pebbles . . . Presently you find a comfortable place on the grassy bank and sit down beside the water. As you reach forward you place your fingers in the stream and feel the fresh cool water

running past your fingers . . . You feel so peaceful, so relaxed.

3 You lean back comfortably against the trunk of a big tree and think about a relationship that you want to improve. Think about the person who is important to you in this relationship and as you do so ask yourself: *How important is this relationship to me? Why am I in this relationship? What do I need from this person?* Think about the way this relationship helps you. Take your time to do this thoroughly . . . Now consider those areas in your life where you feel your feelings and needs are not understood. Is there part of you not being satisfied or fulfilled?

4 Now consider the other person in this relationship. What do you think they need from you? Do you *really know* what they want? Do you satisfy them? Do you fulfil their needs? Have you perhaps stopped making as much effort or taking as much interest as you did in your early days together? Ask yourself: *In what way can things be improved between us?*

5 As you continue to relax beside the stream, imagine this person appearing in the distance. You wave and call out their name. This person comes to join you. You look closely at the familiar face, recalling the good things you have shared. You remember how it was when you were first together. You begin to communicate as you never have before, without any desire to get back at this person or to defend yourself. You really want to find out what he/she needs from you. Feel the relationship grow. Feel a caring within you for this other person's happiness. Share your own thoughts. Explain your own feelings, your own needs.

6 Decide now to speak with this person about these things at a conscious level when next you have the

opportunity to do so. Fulfil your own desire to improve the relationship.

7   When you have learned all you can from this experience, say quietly to yourself: *I will do all that I can to improve things between us. Our relationship is going to grow better and better.*

8   Count slowly backwards from five to one, open your eyes, look around the room and have a good stretch. Feel optimistic about your ability to communicate and improve that relationship.

9

Dealing with Jealousy, Envy and Guilt

Jealousy

This emotion is so powerful that it can completely destroy the person who is unfortunate enough to experience it. Creeping in insidiously, often with no foundation, jealousy twists and distorts the mind as if it has a will of its own. Intense feelings of jealousy can end up destroying that which the jealous person wants so desperately to preserve.

This emotion can change a person's true personality out of all recognition. Feelings may become so obsessive that the person completely loses touch with reality.

Consider the dictionary's definition of jealousy: 'fearful of being supplanted; apprehensive of loss of position or affection . . .' Most feelings of jealousy are about someone being the giver or recipient of feelings or favours that the jealous person wants for him or herself. When we know absolutely that we cannot have a certain person's affections, or when we are not prepared to share them, the resultant emotions are often those of bitterness, revenge, or even hatred.

Many acts of crime have been committed through jealousy. A man (or woman) will sometimes destroy the person he professes to love, rather than let another have those affections he is convinced should belong only to him. We read of it daily in the national newspapers.

Nothing good ever came of jealousy. So why do we experience it? Where does it come from? It doesn't appear to fit into our survival programme. Again we have to look back to our childhood. Most forms of jealousy are unwittingly caused by parents or teachers. A first child, pushed aside for the 'new baby', is going to feel tremendous anger, fear and rejection. Hearing praise or seeing favours heaped on another cannot fail to fire feelings of frustration, resentment and hurt.

Sibling rivalry is a common source of jealousy. The situation is made worse, and feelings intensified, when the jealous person recognizes that the brother or sister he/she loves, is responsible for those bad feelings. The confusion and conflict are often impossible to reconcile.

To avoid dealing with emotions that we do not like, we often transfer them to someone else. So long as we can hate qualities or emotions in another, we do not have to face them within ourselves. When we denounce someone for being inconsiderate, selfish, mean, ungrateful, we are, in effect, saying that of course *we* are not like that.

A bewildered father told me that his younger son had accused him of treating his elder brother with preference. To support his belief he had even counted the photographs taken of them as children; he noted that there were more pictures of the first son. The father explained that this almost always happened with a first child, until you realized that you were taking dozens of almost identical pictures. The younger son refused to consider this as a valid explanation. He went on to look for more evidence to support his belief. He was convinced that he was, and always had been, unfairly treated. Such an attitude will cause a child to become sulky, resentful, sullen and extremely difficult to handle.

A bad teacher can, in trying to stimulate pupils to greater effort, set up a 'model' child as an example. This only serves to create feelings of jealousy or envy, with angry resentment bubbling beneath the surface: *Why didn't she choose me? Why can't I be clever like him? I wish I had her hair! It's favouritism!*

Of course a teacher electing a child as an example can be the spur to greater effort, but all too often this treatment only breeds resentment and jealousy. Most children appear to grow out of it. They develop their own skills, interests and friends, so that being who they are feels okay.

But growing up and falling in love and experiencing the fear of losing or having to share the affections of the one who has become so all-important, can result in a re-stimulation of those old emotions. The same feelings of jealousy can appear in a work situation, between friends, even in sport.

There can be tremendous conflict between the logical Left Brain and the emotional Right Brain over jealousy. Women clients, aware of this conflict, have confessed to me that jealousy is ruining their lives. 'I know he isn't really having an affair,' they tell me. 'But I keep creating these pictures of him with another woman. I don't want to let him out of my sight.' They know all too well that such behaviour is driving their loved one away, but they seem incapable of doing anything about it.

All the joy in those relationships is spoiled by these uncontrollable feelings. It is easy to see here that the underlying problem is fear: fear of losing the loved one, fear of rejection, fear of being alone. The sooner such feelings are dealt with the better.

Exercise 9 – Resolving Feelings of Jealousy

Note: Having used some of the previous exercises, you may now find that you can quickly and easily achieve alpha level without the need to go through a complete relaxation exercise. In the following exercise I have given a shortened version for you to try. You can, of course, still use one of the other inductions if you choose, or you may select one from those listed at the end of this book.

1 Make yourself comfortable and relax. Look across the room and focus your eyes on something in front of you. Keep looking at that spot until you begin to experience a day-dreaming kind of feeling. Your eyes will de-focus and you will feel as if you are staring into space. Now close your eyes and note your physical responses as you let go and relax. Begin to recognize your own physical feelings telling you that you have reached alpha level.

2 Imagine that you are sitting in a comfortable arm chair and in front of you is a coffee table. On the table are a number of coloured boxes. Inside each box is a jigsaw puzzle portraying some part of your past that is responsible for causing you to feel jealous. You can choose to open any one of these boxes. Do that now. Select a colour, open the lid and tip the pieces out onto the table . . . As you do this, quietly ask yourself: *Where did this feeling of jealousy come from? What first caused me to feel this way? How did it happen?* . . . Now fit the pieces of the puzzle together. As you do so a picture emerges portraying something from your past that caused those original feelings of jealousy. You begin to understand the origin of your fears, why you felt jealous.

3 As you look at this picture you recognize that those feelings belong to the past. You are more mature now.

You can understand and forgive . . . you can let go of the past. Now break up the puzzle and cast it aside . . .

If you feel there is more than one event responsible for those feelings of anxiety, those jealous feelings, take another box of a different colour and build the next puzzle . . . You view it with understanding, then break it up and cast it aside. There are more boxes there if you need them. Deal with them in the same way.

4 There is still one box you hadn't noticed until now. It is on the floor beneath the table, wrapped in golden paper and tied with silver ribbons. You lift it onto the table feeling a deep curiosity. What is inside? As you open the lid and tip up the box, another puzzle falls out onto the table. This is a picture of your future. A wonderful positive picture of yourself, freed from all those old bad feelings of jealousy. You fit the pieces together, gaining a new understanding, a new way of looking at yourself and your life that is positive and productive. Enjoy the feelings you experience as you view your future self . . . See yourself now acting and responding in a way that feels good, completely free from those past jealous feelings.

5 Count slowly backwards from five to one, and as you do so open your eyes and return to full conscious awareness, feeling relaxed, refreshed and in control.

Note: Sometimes there is justification for feeling that you cannot trust a loved one, that they are being unfaithful – in a case like this you will have to decide whether the person is really worth all the feelings of anxiety and fear. It may be that you need to change your view of that person. Often our feelings are based on how we want to perceive a person, and we fail, or refuse to see them as they really are.

Caution: Some women experience such powerful feelings

of jealousy over another woman's baby that they will attempt to steal or destroy the child. *This problem most definitely needs professional help.*

In any situation where there are excessive feelings of violence or destruction, the help of a professional therapist or doctor is strongly advised.

Envy

Envy is the powerful longing to possess that which someone else has. This may take the form of coveting someone else's house, car, jewellery, job, and so on. So long as it is a materialistic thing, then there is no reason why motivation and effort cannot turn the longing into a reality.

Envying the attributes or character of another person needs to be dealt with in a different way. We cannot have someone else's personality, their sense of humour, or the respect they receive from others. We may develop similar attributes, but as each of us is unique, we cannot take on the personality of another.

Seeing qualities that are attractive in someone else can motivate us to change. However, the desire to change should be prompted by wanting to become a better or improved person in our own right, not by trying to be someone else.

Most envy is a wistful longing for things that, in reality, require too much effort or dedication to attain for ourselves.

Envy can result from total discontent. It seems that no matter what people in this mental state possess, it is never enough and any alternative becomes a focus for envy.

There are areas in life where we should, for our own peace of mind, and for those whose lives are affected by our behaviour, learn to appreciate what we have and be satisfied.

If you experience envy, define it. What exactly do you envy? Is it the possessing of something materialistic? Is it the social position you believe goes with that possession? Do you think that having this thing will bring you happiness? Why do you want that thing? What would it achieve?

You may envy a very successful business person, but would you be prepared to shoulder the responsibilities, the pressures, the lack of freedom that such a position brings?

Once you really look at what you are envying it becomes easy to do something about it.

- You can work towards attaining a similar goal.

- You can recognize it is not, in reality, what you want or need – in which case you change your viewpoint.

- You can recognize that it is not possible (we are not all capable of being opera singers or Olympic athletes) and select a new attainable goal – one that is more exciting, more challenging, more rewarding than your existing position. The old envy will then fade into insignificance.

Exercise 10 – Dealing with Envy

1 Make yourself comfortable and relax. Look across the room, focus your eyes on something in front of you. Keep looking at that spot until you begin to experience a day-dreaming feeling. Begin to feel as if you are staring into space. Let your eyes gently close and concentrate on your own physical feelings, recognizing your own signals telling you that you are deeply relaxed – at alpha level.

2 Picture yourself in a beautiful, peaceful place where you will not be interrupted. This can be in a room in your

own house, in a private luxury room in a hotel overlooking a beach, in a garden or woodland . . . Take your time to picture your surroundings, noticing any sounds, smells, the texture of things . . .

3 In your relaxed state consider that which you envy. Look behind the feeling of envy. What is it that you really desire? Wanting to have a fantastic physique may indicate your longing to be admired. You may never, even with years of muscle-building exercises, be able to achieve that likeness. There are, however, other ways of gaining attention and admiration. Stalin had a withered arm, Roosevelt was a cripple, a boy on artificial legs walked across Canada – see what they achieved! You may envy the perfect teeth of someone you know. There's no way you can have teeth like that (though you may be able to disguise those you do have), but there is nothing preventing you from having a smile that is even more attractive. You may envy someone who has a lot of money, a new car or a large house, you may envy someone's popularity . . .

4 Identify the core of your envy. Then ask your unconscious mind to take responsibility for making those changes necessary so that you no longer experience those negative feelings. Do this quietly now in your own way . . . Decide whether you are prepared to make the effort required to reach a similar position or goal. Recognize that it is up to you – see how you can set about achieving this aim . . .

5 While at alpha level, picture some of the positives in your own life. This may be difficult at first if you have been in the habit of thinking that others have more, or are better than you. But you *do* have attractive qualities that belong essentially to you, and there *are* things you can enjoy and feel pleased about. Enhance them with your imagination . . .

6 When you are ready, and you have enjoyed this positive experience, count slowly backwards from five to one, open your eyes and return to full conscious awareness feeling much more content and happy within yourself.

Note: Repeat this exercise daily over the next few days.

Where you have decided to achieve a similar goal, focus often on it – in this way you will strengthen your determination and desire to achieve.

Guilt

Guilt is learned as a child. We cannot escape it. There are times in our development when each of us is 'made to feel guilty'. It is a response to conditioning by those in authority within our society.

Even when we are very young we are made to feel guilty if we disobey or break the rules. Making us feel guilty is a way of control – it gives power to the person who creates the guilty response. Religion, parents, friends, neighbours, colleagues, the law, the media – all play their part in the guilt game. We would never know how to feel bad about something unless someone had taught us, either by words or example.

Feeling guilty about some past deed, error or omission, results in the powerful desire to go back and do that thing differently. We want to go back and change history, but of course we can't. The only good thing about guilt is that we can learn from that experience so that we know not to do it again.

When we do something wrong we are made to feel guilty. Often there is the threat of love being withdrawn: *You will make Mummy angry if you do that. Now you've made Daddy sad. I won't love you anymore if* . . . Even worse, you may be told that you are responsible for making someone ill – giving Mummy a headache – all because you did something you were not supposed to do.

We develop a conscience – a painful but very necessary thing. Somehow we have to be made to abide by the rules if we are going to fit into a civilized society.

Whatever it is that we have done which results in feelings of guilt, we are, in some way, made to feel we have committed a crime. And when we've committed some crime, we expect to be punished. It's all part of the conditioning, the need for someone to have control.

If we weren't afraid of punishment, if we weren't taught to feel guilty, there would have to be another way of commanding respect and obedience.

Some parents know it instinctively – obedience that is motivated through love. What a wonderful world it would be if everyone's behaviour was controlled by love for their fellow man! Unfortunately we do not live in a perfect world and punishment, or the threat of punishment, seems a shorter route to obedience and control.

The restrictions brought about by this sense of guilt do, however, depend on where we are born and raised. In Western civilization, breaking your child's limbs would most certainly be seen as a wicked crime, and some form of punishment would follow. In poor, third-world countries (at least until recent times), turning your child into a cripple by inflicting injury would ensure his survival, for as a cripple he could always beg. This demonstrates that what is right or wrong is determined entirely by our culture.

When we feel we have done something wrong we expect to be punished. If punishment does not follow we set about punishing ourselves – we feel guilty. We begin to believe we don't deserve happiness, success, friends, kindness. Sometimes we behave in a way that drives people from us. All to no avail. The guilty feelings continue.

There is only one way to rid yourself of guilt – no one else can do it for you. *You have to forgive yourself.*

How Do You Forgive Yourself?

You first need to recognize that we all do our best at the time. You may not think so, but given the same circumstances, the same emotions, the same pressures, the state of your physical and mental health at the time, your lack of experience or wisdom, you did the only thing you could do at that moment in your life.

The fact that you now wish you could go back and change things, is a measure of your maturity – you have developed and evolved. That you now experience feelings of guilt is an indication of how much you have progressed as a caring human being.

You did not fail. There is no such thing as failure, only learned experiences. Learning from past experiences is a positive step towards growth. You don't need to keep reminding yourself. Placed in similar circumstances, you can be sure your unconscious mind will remind you not to do it again, for guilt is a painful emotion and you want to avoid it.

If, however, the guilt causes only a small degree of discomfort, then you are likely to repeat the act until the build-up of guilt feelings is such that you will do anything to prevent them continuing.

There are only two ways to eliminate guilt.

- You forgive yourself.

- You do not repeat the act.

There are some people who believe that the only way to overcome feelings of guilt is to confess the deed or bad thoughts. This is a convenient way of off-loading guilt but it does not always help the person on the other end of the confession. When considering this road, ask yourself what is your true intention? If it is to make yourself more comfortable, and/or if your confession is going to cause pain or heartache to another, you need to follow another route. Some people find the solution in religion, others seek to punish themselves in some way. The answer can simply be to learn from that experience, vow never to do such a thing again, and *forgive yourself*.

A lovely lady once confessed to me that when she was a child she had stolen a pencil from a shop. Although she realized it was the kind of thing children do, she had never been able to let go of the feeling of guilt. She knew she could simply go to the shop and pay for the pencil (it was only a few pence), but she still didn't believe this would enable her to let go of the bad feeling. 'Every time I go near the store I am reminded of it,' she confessed. Obviously paying over the money will not make the slightest difference to the store, but forgiving herself will release her from this futile feeling.

Bereavement

Bereavement is perhaps responsible for more feelings of guilt than any other experience. Even the most attentive and dutiful children, when bereaved, can be seen berating themselves over some past deed or omission. No matter how kind, thoughtful or caring they have been, they will focus on the one occasion they didn't do something; they remind themselves over and over again of that time when they became impatient, frustrated or acted thoughtlessly. It seems almost as if the more they did for the person who has died, the more guilt they experience.

The answer to this seems to lie in an inability to let go. While they are experiencing those powerful feelings of guilt – no matter how painful – they are still in contact. That person is, in a way, still with them.

There is a better way of being in touch and that is through the rekindling of past good memories, the happy occasions, the laughter shared. But guilt tends to override all this and the sense of despair and desolation can become unbearable.

To let the good memories surface, and to enjoy them, it is necessary to remind yourself that you are only human, with all the frailties and weaknesses of every other human being. Acknowledge this and forgive yourself.

I recently read a note from an old lady to her family. It said, *Don't grieve when I am gone, remember the happy times we shared.* Surely it is what your loved one would want – for you to be happy and to hold on to all that was good in that relationship.

Guilt, fear and sin are all products of your imagination. As you focus on them, you strengthen those pictures supporting your beliefs about yourself and you respond emotionally. To forgive yourself you need to use your image-making capacity in a positive way.

Try gradually moving those negative pictures that cause re-stimulation of sad feelings until they are behind you. This will allow you to focus on more positive, happy occasions when you recall the person you have lost.

Exercise 11 – Eliminating Guilt

1   Gently close your eyes and take a deep, deep breath; really fill your lungs with air and then breathe out and relax. Continue breathing deeply and evenly and as you do so notice any jerkiness or unevenness in your breathing and try to smooth it out . . .

2 As you continue breathing deeply and evenly imagine that each breath you take in is like a swing going up into the air, and as you exhale the swing comes back down again . . .

3 Mentally create your surroundings. Your swing can be in any place you choose: in a familiar garden or one from your own imagination, it may be in a park or tied to a tree in an old orchard . . . You may like to imagine you are a child again sitting on the swing, or perhaps you are pushing someone else . . . As you continue breathing deeply in and out, imagine what you can see as you look up . . . a clear blue sky overhead with an aeroplane high above you, its wings shining silver in the sunlight. Perhaps you hear birds or the sound of children's voices as they play. You may be able to see over the tree tops, you may see roof tops or a distant church spire . . .

4 Breathe deeply and evenly and as you do so notice any physical discomfort: it may be in your lower back, in your neck or shoulders . . . When you have located it, calmly acknowledge it . . .

5 Now as you breathe in, imagine that you are feeding oxygen directly to that area – life-giving oxygen, cleansing and healing – and as you breathe out you release any stress or tension, you just let it melt away . . .

6 Continue in this way for a few minutes until you feel comfortably relaxed . . . Now begin to mentally check over your body starting with your feet. Think of each toe in turn, first on one foot and then on the other . . . By this time you will notice that you can hardly feel some of your toes at all and that you can barely distinguish one toe from the next . . . Notice the feelings in your legs as you let go and relax. They begin to feel so heavy, so heavy and relaxed. That's fine, just let all

of your muscles go on and on relaxing . . . Continue checking over your body as you feel your stomach muscles relax, your chest, your back . . . Notice the rhythm of your breathing . . . it has slowed down. You may even be able to feel your heart beating as you let go and relax. Let your scalp relax . . . Allow all of the muscles in your face, your mouth and lips to relax. Let your neck and shoulders relax and as you do so imagine all the stress and tension from your head, your neck and shoulders flowing down through your arms and out through the tips of your fingers. Your arms begin to feel heavy as you relax deeper and deeper. Notice the feelings and sensations in your hands and fingers as you relax more and more . . . be aware of any tingling, any throbbing of pulses, any warmth or coldness. Recognize your own signals telling you that you are relaxed, that you are at alpha level.

7 Imagine yourself in a beautiful room that you have created. You had all the money you needed to make this room warm, and comfortable. There is an open fireplace with a crackling log fire in the hearth; some photographs or pictures hang on the walls and there is a bowl of flowers on a polished coffee table – you notice the colour of the flowers – you may even be able to smell the faint perfume from them. You sit in a comfortable armchair in front of the fire and relax . . .

8 Think of an act or some aspect of your behaviour about which you have been feeling guilty. As you do so, see yourself in the distance the way you were at that time . . . With those pressures and emotions you were experiencing, the stress you were under, your state of physical and mental health at that time, you were doing your best. You were younger then. Even if only a few weeks have passed, you were not as mature then as you are now.

9 As you look at that less wise, less mature you, forgive yourself. Imagine if it was someone else in that situation, what would you say to them? How would you comfort them? What would you say to reassure them? . . . Now give yourself the same reassurance, the same words of comfort . . .

10 See the guilt as a bright red-coloured ball. As you watch, it grows smaller and smaller . . . the colour is fading. The ball grows still smaller until it disappears completely . . .

11 Relax and see yourself as you are now, sitting in your own special room. You are at peace with yourself and smiling. You have dealt with past problems and you are freed from them. See this older, wiser you, with so many options and wonderful things in life to do . . .

12 Count slowly backwards from five to one and as you do so, gently open your eyes and return to full conscious awareness, feeling relaxed and at peace.

Note: You can use a shortened induction to reach alpha level if you wish. You would then start this exercise at step 7.

Current Actions that are Causing Feelings of Guilt

If you are currently behaving in a way that makes you feel guilty, this must be dealt with in a different way.

Perhaps you are involved in an 'affair', a dishonest act, hiding the truth, deliberately undermining someone's confidence, remaining silent when you know you should speak out. If something like this is creating in you feelings of guilt, ask yourself: *Why do I do this? Is it essential or necessary? What would happen if I stopped behaving in this way?* Only by asking the right kind of questions can you hope to find satisfactory solutions.

As with all things that involve the emotions, this way of dealing with guilt is better done in a mentally relaxed state.

Go to alpha level and consider all the things associated with that guilt: material or physical things which may be involved in this act; emotions, pressures, stress, the effect upon others. Ask yourself, in continuing with this act, are you right to feel guilty? If the answer to this question is 'yes', there is only one way to eliminate the guilt – stop doing it *now*. It may be hard, it may seem impossible, you may have to make sacrifices, but you have within you the power to change. You have only to want this change and to focus on the positive results. Motivated by the desire to change, to eliminate those feelings of guilt, you can change.

If there is no way you can stop or change what is happening – if you honestly believe this – then you change your point of view. This way, the feelings of guilt are eliminated or at least diminished.

'I'm going to feel guilty after I've eaten this!'

The Guilty Habit

Certain behavioural patterns can become habit. Guilt is one of them. People can become so used to feeling guilty that they look for a reason to feel guilty about almost anything. It's like getting on a roundabout and not knowing how to jump off. They have found a perfect way to feel bad about everything. They rush to take the blame when often it has nothing at all to do with them. This compulsive need to go on punishing themselves can make them feel important; acting this way becomes the reason for their existence.

With such negative people, the only way to help them is to encourage them to participate in things that they can truly enjoy. These should be things which even they can perceive as guiltless. It's hard work. Even enjoying a walk in the sunshine can elicit a response such as 'I feel guilty enjoying this when there are people who have to work or are sick in hospital.'

Asking them what difference it would make if they didn't take the walk may help them to see the futility of such guilty feelings. At least it may make them pause and review the way they are thinking.

But such people, determined to feel guilty, have to *want* to change. When they genuinely admit this, learning to use self-hypnosis and some of the exercises described in this book can help.

10

Overcoming Fears and Phobias

Essential Fear

Fear is part of our survival instinct. Fear warns us when to take action, it gives us the spur we need to act and think quickly. Without this instinctual reaction when we feel threatened, we could not survive. There is nothing we need do about it, only be in tune with ourselves so that we do not ignore it or override it.

If we were not afraid of pain or dying, we would drive around like maniacs; if we had no fear of drowning we would go out of our depth in the sea before we had learned to swim; if we were not afraid of the consequences, we might leap off a high building to find out how it felt. These examples are enough to show that fear is vital to our survival.

No matter how much someone may dare or challenge you, if your instinctual response is to be afraid and your life is threatened, *you have every right to say no*.

There will be occasions when, having weighed up the risks, you decide to do something dangerous anyway, but, having made yourself aware of those dangers, you programme yourself to take whatever precautions are possible to ensure your well-being.

The desire to do something is sometimes so powerful that we will risk our life in order to attain that goal. The aeroplane would never have taken off into the air had someone not dared to risk all – but it was a calculated risk, they expected to survive.

Man has sometimes deliberately given his life for the sake of others, or for his beliefs. This is when the will becomes stronger than the instinct for survival – it is often admirable, sometimes foolhardy, but shows how powerful the mind is.

False Fears

False fears are those which have no apparent foundation and yet have powerful control over the way we act. We receive these fears in several ways.

1 from our parents (or other adults) when we were children

2 by relating to something heard, or read, or seen in a film

3 through superstitious beliefs

4 from an influential authoritative figure

The following examples relate to the above ways in which fears are transmitted.

1 Two young children once stayed overnight in my house. Half an hour after I had put them to bed they reappeared at the top of the stairs, sobbing and hysterical. After calming them, I asked what was the problem. They told me that there was a moth in the bedroom. I explained that moths could not hurt them and asked why were they afraid. 'M-m-mummy is frightened of moths,' they told me.

2 Television, which is so visual, will often lull us into alpha level, and then, as the logical Left Brain relaxes, the imaginative Right Brain responds. By allowing this to happen, we best enjoy the film. Occasionally we experience what we see and hear as if it were actually happening to us. We have all had those moments of experiencing the horror, sadness or fear that belongs to the character portraying it. The problem arises when we experience these emotions as if they were our own. We then become unable to differentiate between reality and fiction.

Case History

A young mother had developed a terrible fear of being separated from her baby. As we talked about the cause of her fear, she recalled that this had begun on the day of her baby's christening. Walking to and from the kitchen with food and drinks for the guests, she had paid no attention to the television. A film was showing a holocaust – the earth was cracking, and screaming, terrified people were being separated, some falling into the widening cracks. At a conscious level she was occupied thinking about the guests, but she had still seen bits of the film and heard the sounds; unconsciously her mind had absorbed the fear. She began to relate emotionally to the story. It seemed to her that she was being torn away from her own baby. These feelings only became evident much later and she failed to connect them to the film.

With the use of hypnosis, she recognized that the fear did not belong to her but to the characters in the film. We then used the visualization technique of 'undoing an experience' as if it had really happened. To her it *was* a reality and this was the way she experienced it. She then created a very strong safe picture of herself with her baby that made her feel secure and happy.

From my experience and observations, I believe that those things to which we do not consciously pay attention are the ones that have the most powerful influence on the emotional part of us.

3 Superstitious beliefs are assimilated from our cultural background. We do not consciously learn them. They become part of our belief system without us ever having logically considered them. In some parts of the world, superstitious beliefs are so powerful that they can cause sickness and even death.

If you are bothered about superstitions, use the technique for 'Talking to Your Unconscious Mind' (Exercise 6). Visualize your unconscious mind as a shape and colour. Hold that image in your mind and ask it to identify those fears that have their origin in superstitious beliefs. Ask your 'unconscious mind image' to recognize they are not valid and that you do not need them in order to survive. Then ask your unconscious mind to take responsibility for removing those fears.

4 Figures in authority can have tremendous influence. Often we believe them simply because of who they are without asking whether they are right or have the knowledge or experience to substantiate their state-ments. The media is a very good example of this. The number of people who believe, without question, every-thing that is fed to them through the media, is quite amazing. Naturally we are going to believe some of it, but relayed 'facts' need to be viewed with caution. Often it is only someone's opinion, or a fact exaggerated or taken out of context in order to make a saleable story.

We are never more influenced by authoritative figures than when we are young and impressionable. Let me share with you a lovely story I had told to me about a little boy called Peter. One day he went into the garden where his father was working. He asked his daddy why he was ploughing up the garden. 'I'm not ploughing it,' his father replied. Peter waited a few minutes and repeated the question. 'I'm not ploughing,' his father said again. Once more there was a pause and then again Peter asked the same question. Exasperated, his father said, 'Why do you think I'm ploughing?' 'Mummy said so,' was the reply. (His father was in reality using a cultivator, which the mother had loosely referred to as a plough!)

We always have the right to question. The person concerned may be important but they are not always right!

False fears are often based on misconceptions. Someone may say 'I'm always ill when there is a thunder-storm – they make me physically sick.'

If we anticipate something and expect it to happen, it usually does. We rarely question why or ask if there is anything we can do to change the way we feel. Perhaps the person 'made ill' by thunder-storms is only sensitive to the build-up of positive ions in the air. An ionizer may be all that is needed to put things right.

How we perceive things, whether they are true or false, is part of our overall belief system. We produce a behaviour pattern that enables us to survive – we get along, we cope.

Exposing the origin of our fears is not something the unconscious mind will readily do, for it means thinking about and exploring that area which has created the emotional reaction. We feel we cannot bear to confront it.

I don't want to think about it and *I can't bear to picture it* are among the usual responses when I ask clients what *exactly* they are afraid of. But all the time, at an unconscious level, they are being reminded. There is no escape. The sooner the fear is reviewed and resolved, the better.

False fears can come from a lack of confidence and from a poor self-image. Building your self-esteem will most certainly help you to deal with these fears. When you are sure of yourself, when you no longer feel the need to please others or to have their approval, you will no longer be afraid. What other people may think about you will no longer concern you.

Irrational Fears

Irrational fears are the ones we could well do without. They frequently limit or spoil our lives.

They have no survival benefits and are those we need to do something about.

Phobias

Phobias are where most of our irrational fears lie. I have yet to meet anyone who does not have a phobia about something. Often it is not important, it does not restrict their lives and they can get along without doing anything about it. Or they may refuse to accept that they *can* do something to change their responses and continue to hold on to their phobia. What we are considering here are phobias that *do* affect your life and that you would like to deal with.

A phobia is an overwhelming fear or dread of something. Instead of decreasing in intensity, each time the victim has a similar experience (or reminder) it seems to grow worse. It becomes an exaggerated irrational response to something seen as a threat.

We can develop a phobia about almost anything: spiders, water, heights, lightning, space, birds, snakes, rats, going out shopping, flying – even buttons. It comes from the belief that this 'thing' is in some way threatening us, and the brain, by controlling our reactions, prevents us from facing the threat and having to deal with it.

Things that the unconscious mind sees as threatening, may not, in reality, be harmful. Of course there are dangerous spiders, but not naturally in the British Isles, and yet this is one of the most common phobias there.

There is always a cause. From an initial experience, where you were not able to rationalize immediately, you became frightened. Your survival response went into action long before you had time to pause and evaluate the situation. Once a behaviour pattern has been established, it will be repeated time and time again. This response, however inconvenient, has enabled you to survive and you look no further.

Phobic responses are frequently learned as children, but can occur at any time in life. Sometimes they come from an isolated incident – it takes only seconds to develop a phobia.

All fear starts in the mind. The emotional response takes place as the mind replays the past event. This response is immediate and will go into action whenever there is a reminder of that experience.

'Why do I always anticipate things going wrong?'

A phobic reaction seems to have nothing to do with choice. It is as if you are 'taken over' by something more powerful.

The first step to dealing with a phobia is to find out why you have it. This may sound odd, but some phobias do have a 'secondary gain'. By this I mean that they enable something beneficial to happen.

Many women that I have counselled admit to being afraid of going out alone, and believe they are suffering from claustrophobia. It may have started one day at the superstore check-out perhaps they discovered they had left their purse behind, or they were feeling very hot and feared they were going to faint; they may, quite suddenly, have needed a toilet and felt afraid that they wouldn't get there in time. Behind all these fears is the *real* fear of showing themselves up in front of others, of losing control. Whatever the cause, it results in them being afraid to go out alone.

Okay, so that looks like a straightforward phobia. But it isn't always so. When I hear a client say, 'I can't go anywhere without my husband now. He even has to come to the shops with me,' I know it is necessary to look beneath the surface.

The wife, who may have felt neglected – perhaps left at home whilst the husband went out and about pursuing his own interests – has found a perfect way of keeping him near her. She is not going to let that phobia go in a hurry! The secondary gain is too important to her and she, quite genuinely, is not aware of what is happening.

If this proves to be the case, then it becomes necessary first to deal with the relationship and to find ways in which the couple can improve communication. She must also build her own ego so that she will, hopefully, pursue hobbies and interests of her own. *Then* she can deal with the phobia.

Case History

Joan was 73 when I met her. She had a very powerful phobia concerning the wind. If it was forecast above gale force three she insisted on her bed being brought downstairs and she would hide beneath the covers trembling. She listened to every weather forecast and was afraid most of the time to go out in case the wind force increased. Joan's husband was fed up with her. He spent most of his time in a work shed at the bottom of the garden choosing not to hear her and her 'complaints'.

It was quite a simple matter to find what had caused the fear: when she was a little girl she could see from her bedroom window a very tall chimney stack swaying in the wind. Joan was afraid that one night a strong wind would blow it down. She used to imagine it crashing through her window.

My usual methods of dealing with her phobia did nothing to diminish her fears. I dug deeper and discovered that she had two adult children who now lived away from home. Whenever a strong wind was forecast they would phone to check she was all right. Usually one of them would drive over to stay with her.

Joan had never come to terms with her family growing up and leaving home. Failing to develop inner resources or independent interests meant that she still needed her children. Her phobia – certainly genuine – ensured that they kept coming back. Had she been younger, or if her husband had been prepared to co-operate, we could have made progress. But Joan was too old and set in her ways to make changes. She chose to keep her phobia and stopped attending the clinic.

There are, of course, many phobias which are straight-forward and their only achievement is that they prevent the victim from doing that thing again. Going to the dentist is a good example of this. If you had a bad time on your last visit – maybe your reaction was greatly exaggerated, out of all proportion to the original experience – you will keep putting off the next visit. How then are you going to deal with this kind of fear so that future treatments are not viewed with dread, or even terror?

When you use the following exercise, apply it to your own particular phobia.

Exercise 12 – Dealing with Phobias

1 Make yourself comfortable and relax. Look across the room and focus your eyes on something in front of you. Anything will do – a picture, a mark on the wall, a lamp . . . As you continue to focus on that spot, begin slowly counting backwards from 500 quietly to yourself . . . Continue counting until you feel your eyes getting tired and wanting to close. As soon as they feel ready to close, let them do so. Don't struggle to keep them open, they will naturally begin to feel tired or watery and start to blink. Let everything happen naturally.

2 When your eyes have closed, stop counting and mentally check that each part of your body is completely relaxed. Feel your toes relax, your legs, your body . . . Allow a calm, peaceful expression to pass across your face; let your mouth and lips relax. Imagine all the stress and tension from your head, neck and shoulders flowing down your arms and out through the tips of your fingers. Be comfortably aware of the feelings and sensations in your body as you relax to alpha level.

3 Identify your phobia. Ask yourself: *Does it have a secondary gain? Does it allow something to happen that is more important to me?* If the answer is 'yes', you must deal with

the secondary gain first. If you don't, it will only manifest itself in some other way. (Should you feel that you can't handle this yourself, see a therapist.) First, you may like to try using the 'Talking to Your Unconscious Mind' technique, detailed in Exercise 6, to identify the secondary gain behind the phobia. If there is no secondary gain and you see yours as a straightforward phobia, you can now deal with it.

4 Picture yourself going into an empty cinema. You can imagine someone with you if you feel better that way. You make your way between the seats until you are roughly in the centre and you then pull down a seat, sit on it, and look at the screen. On the screen you create a picture of yourself just before you experience your phobic response. See this picture in black and white, a bit faded perhaps so that it is not too clear. If you can recall when it happened, what caused your fear, then go back to that first occasion. If you have no memory of where it came from or how it started, use the pictures that come into your mind when you think of your phobia. What, exactly, do you imagine is going to happen? Even if, in reality, it has never happened, use the pictures of what you imagine *might* happen. These can be just as powerful in causing a phobia. You may picture the plane in which you fly crashing – it hasn't done so because fear may have prevented you from ever leaving the ground, but use those pictures, imagined or real.

5 With the 'just before' picture of yourself on the screen, imagine that you float up from your seat into the projection room. From here you can look down and see yourself still sitting in the seat. You can also still see that picture of yourself on the screen. (Putting yourself in the projection room in this way helps you to separate yourself from the experience you are about to watch.) You have the controls in your hand and can switch the

pictures on or off as you choose. It is not necessary to imagine yourself going through that phobic experience again, you need only to picture it from a distance. If you think it may still feel too real, visualize a glass panel or filter between you and the cinema screen. You now press the controls and turn it into a film. Watch it right through to just beyond the end and then press the pause button.

6 Now imagine that you press another button and turn that picture into colour. You now jump *into* the picture and run it backwards. Everything happens in reverse. Take just a few seconds to do this. (Quietly tell yourself what is happening as you do this, if you find that it helps.)

7 Open your eyes and take note of your surroundings. Pause for a few moments then close them again. Now picture yourself without the phobia, feeling completely free to do whatever you choose. Without the phobia what can you now do? Adjust this new positive picture of yourself until it looks and feels good. (If you still have any doubts repeat the whole process, speeding up the part where you are in the picture and running it backwards.)

8 Now count slowly backwards from five to one, open your eyes and return to full conscious awareness and feel really pleased with your new-found confidence.

Note: This visual exercise can be done by imagining yourself watching the television screen in your own home with exactly the same results. However, if it is a really powerful phobia, using the cinema screen and removing yourself to the projection room will give you a sense of distance and control.

It is essential, when you reverse the picture, to actually imagine yourself physically *in* the picture and not just watching yourself. You won't experience fear when doing this for you are *undoing* the experience, *not* going through it.

If you have several experiences relating to the same phobia, it may be necessary to use this visual exercise with each one in turn. Usually I find that if the client knows where the phobia began, and deals with that, the fear disappears.

I have used this technique to help cure hundreds of phobias and I have never known it to fail with a straightforward phobia, if done properly.

Thinking about the things you can do when you no longer have that phobia (or fear) will give you a sense of positive expectation. If your phobia is one of flying, being free of that fear means that you can take a holiday abroad. When spiders don't bother you, you will be able to pop them into an empty jar and shake them out of the window. When you aren't afraid of water you can learn to swim. Positive expectation of something good happening gives you courage.

It is far better to deal with fear than to deny it.

'*If only I didn't have this phobia about flying!*'

11

Coping With Anger

Anger

We can all feel angry sometimes. Anger can be useful, constructive or destructive, a way of communicating something is very wrong. If we deny this emotion and fail to deal with it, deep and lasting problems can arise.

Anger is one of our most powerful emotions. We have only to look in the newspapers to read of the effects of uncontrollable anger; child battering, maiming, destruction of property, war and death can all result from this emotion. It seems to take over completely, driving a person to behave outside reasonable or normal behaviour. Knowing that the punishment for such an act can be life imprisonment, confinement in a psychiatric ward, even death, does not deter. 'Blind with anger' is indeed a true expression.

The frightening truth is that if another human being is capable of such actions then so are we. Even the most law-abiding gentle people can suddenly be possessed by these powerful feelings, driving them to act in a way totally out of character.

Anger that Supports the Survival System

In a small sub post office in the West of England, an intruder was physically attacking the owner when his daughter walked in. She had been sweeping the floor outside and still carried the broom. Without any thought for her safety, she set about the attacker with the broom. He fled, leaving his loot behind. When interviewed by the press she was asked if she hadn't been frightened at the time. To this she replied, 'I was too angry to be afraid when I saw what he was doing to my father.'

This kind of anger, overriding caution or fear, comes to our aid at the right time. It can give us that extra motivation, sending a surge of adrenaline racing through the body that prompts instant action.

Anger of this kind prevents us feeling afraid. We do not need to stop and question it, or ask whether it is right or wrong – it just is.

When Anger is Justified

There are times when anger is justified. We are right to feel anger over injustices, intimidation, corruption of people in authority, cruelty to children or animals. When we hear of food and medical supplies, intended for starving innocent people, being commandeered for the soldiers responsible for causing those conditions of hunger and hardship, then we should feel angry. Anger, in this context, ought to motivate us to try to do something about the situation.

When Anger is Denied

Anger, especially during our formative years, can be a healthy outlet for tension and certain emotions. We need to learn how to express and control anger while we are in a safe, loving, caring environment.

If we are taught that anger is a 'bad thing', frowned upon by those whom we love, even resulting in some kind of punishment, we learn to deny it. We are made to feel that it is wrong to get angry.

Usually, if you are one of those people who finds it difficult to express anger, you probably find it easier not to confront the issue.

As a result of not learning how to deal positively with anger, you do the opposite. Demonstrating it negatively, you eventually explode or yell or smash something. But this achieves nothing – no one is likely to do anything about such angry outbursts. In response, people may shrug, suggest you need a holiday, yell back or tell you to grow up. No one realizes what it is all about. You have still failed to communicate the underlying cause.

Many women find that if they try to demonstrate how much they are upset, how angry they are really feeling inside, they are accused of overreacting or being hysterical and irrational. The situation seems hopeless. They creep back into their old repressed role, feeling miserable and defeated. By not communicating our anger clearly and identifying it precisely, we elicit impatience rather than understanding.

The man (or woman) who finds that conditions at work are frequently causing him to lose his temper, would achieve far more if he expressed the reasons for his frustration instead of yelling and getting everyone's back up.

Futile Anger

Futile anger has nothing to do with injustices or survival anger. It is energy consuming and a total waste of emotions for it achieves nothing positive or good.

We often feel angry when we think we have been overlooked, ignored or treated badly. People who fail to give us the consideration or respect to which we believe we have a right can make us furious.

We can all feel this kind of anger when someone pushes in front of us in a queue, or they pinch the parking space we were just about to reverse into. Something inside us is saying, 'Who does he think he is? How dare he do this to me?' And yet we don't even know that person. It's actually nothing to do with us personally. Maybe the offender really is in a great hurry; perhaps he didn't even notice you were there first. He may be rude and bad mannered but that is his problem. This kind of behaviour just isn't worth getting angry over.

If you really feel that something should be done about such a situation it is better to channel your energy into controlled assertiveness. You can politely say, 'Excuse me, I was first' or 'Please go ahead, you are obviously in a greater hurry than I am.' Or you can simply choose to see the offender as an ill-mannered person and ignore his behaviour.

Whichever way you choose to deal with such a situation, you have taken control and no longer feel the victim. It's a great feeling! Unless anger is dealt with in this way it turns inwards, festering in the mind long after the incident is over – as in the following example.

On the way to work some idiot damn near kills you, swerving out in front of you in his car. You experience a scary moment and become furious with the driver, but there is no way of stopping him and telling him what you think of his driving.

When you arrive at work, the thought is still bubbling inside your head. You need to release the tension but there's no way you can take it out on anyone in the office, you need their co-operation. So you return home still seething.

It has spoilt your whole day and you still want to take it out on someone. The first person you meet when you arrive home and open the front door is most likely to receive the verbal abuse you longed to use that morning. You find yourself saying something like: 'For Christ's sake, why do you always have to have the central heating on? Don't you ever consider the bills?'

Futile, angry feelings that simmer away just under the surface can result in a permanent state of bad temper or irritability. This often makes people belligerent; they seem to be constantly looking for an argument and believe that everyone is against them. They have to believe this, for to accept responsibility for their own behaviour, to believe it is their fault, could further reduce their self-esteem. What good can it achieve? No one and nothing *makes* you angry – you choose the way you respond. 'Don't make me angry,' is a way of putting the responsibility onto someone else and allows you to avoid making your own choices.

Many years ago, remonstrating with my four-year-old son, I told him, 'I don't want to have to get angry with you.' 'Well, don't then,' he replied. I learned a lot from that moment. I had a choice: there were other ways to teach discipline, there were other ways of resolving the problem.

The only way to deal with futile anger is to recognize it for what it is – an energy-consuming, pointless response.

The Angry Habit

Anger can become a habit. Some people respond to almost every adverse situation by getting angry. It often seems to them the only way, but it rarely gets a positive response; it may get things done but it leaves bad feelings. No one responds willingly to angry instructions or orders. Being pleasant and reasonable but firm requires less energy and achieves far more.

In business we want to help the pleasant customer or colleague and we try to avoid the one who constantly flies off into a rage.

Feelings of anger start in our childhood. Wise parents will recognize the necessity for children to express this emotion and learn to control it. Unfortunately, so many adults, never having learned how to deal with their own anger, simply cannot cope with it in their children.

A child, dependent upon his parents for love, security and nourishment, forbidden to question the authority of adults, has to find some way of discharging the build-up of tension. He dare not violate the rules for fear of losing their love, but feelings of anger and frustration have to find an outlet. He may not punch Dad but he can kick the door; he can throw everything out of the drawers onto the floor; he can smash something that he knows they value – then let them try and put that together again!

As adults we often hold on to these behavioural responses from our childhood, never having found a more adequate way of dealing with opposition or frustration.

Being destructive seems to satisfy something inside us. Afterwards come the feelings of remorse: How could I have been so stupid? The feelings turn inwards. We feel childish and disgusted with ourselves – and all this helps to tear our self-esteem apart.

When we are angry it is almost always because the full responsibility for the act, omission or whatever, is seen as being that of someone else. It is no use trying to deal with your temper or wild outbursts when you are feeling like this. They need to be dealt with rationally at quieter, calmer moments.

The decision to do something positive about yourself can only come from you!

Fulfilling a Need

When we have a very poor opinion of ourselves we need constant reassurance that we are okay, that the way we act is acceptable. When this doesn't happen our lack of belief in ourselves is confirmed.

Feeling confident means that we are not bothered by other people's treatment of us – we simply see it as their opinion, or bad manners, or lack of understanding, and we are not affected by it. As the title of one book says: *What You Think of Me is None of My Business*.

Coping With Other People's Anger

When you are confronted by someone who is *very* angry, when they are obviously looking for a row or fight and using something/anything as an excuse, it is necessary to diffuse the situation in the quickest way you can. When someone is furious, it's no use trying to argue your case, or to make them see that perhaps the fault may be theirs. They blame you entirely and you become the focus of all their frustration and pent-up feelings.

Such people are usually beyond reason. You may have quite innocently taken precedence in a situation in the office, inadvertently trimmed the top half of the next-door-neighbour's hedge, forgotten to invite a colleague to a celebration – it could be almost anything.

Often the wisest thing is to accept responsibility: 'I'm sorry.' 'I apologise.' 'I didn't intend to upset you.' It has to be absolute, without qualification. It is simply no use, when someone is extremely angry to say, 'I'm sorry, but

Say quietly to yourself, 'I am in control.'

you really should have been looking . . .' or 'I apologise, but I didn't know . . .'

They are not interested in what you have to say – they have a driving need to hit out at somebody and believe that you have given them the perfect reason to do so.

Much of the wanton destruction in our world today is the result of angry young people wanting to hit out at a society they believe doesn't care a damn about their situation. They have yet to discover that only they can change, for change must come first from within. Unemployment and poor conditions were far more evident in the 1930s but young people didn't go around then smashing up other people's property or assaulting the elderly.

Studies undertaken by Crime Research show that people with low self-esteem do seem to become victims more often than suggested by the law of averages. They are much more likely to be attacked; somehow they seem to send out signals and their body language is unconsciously read by the assailant.

Confident, quietly assertive people do the opposite; they naturally command attention and respect. A bully will think twice before accosting someone whom they feel is superior, whether that strength is of a physical or mental nature.

Exercise 13 – Dealing with Anger

1 (Try using this shortened version to go to alpha level.) Make yourself comfortable and relax. Look across the room, choose something in front of you and focus your eyes on it. Keep looking at that spot until you begin to experience a day-dreaming feeling. Your eyes de-focus and you begin to feel as if you are staring into space. As soon as you become aware of this, let your eyes gently close and concentrate on your own physical feelings. Note your own signals telling you that you are deeply relaxed – at alpha level.

2 Think about something that makes (or made) you feel angry. Anger, particularly against those nearest to us, is often a signal that we are feeling hurt.

3 Identify the real cause of your anger. What are you really angry about? Is it because someone has treated you badly, taken you for granted? Have they blamed you unfairly? Has your privacy been violated? Have you or your family been unjustly criticized or accused? Why exactly are you feeling angry? . . . (Anger can often mask something which goes much deeper.)

4 Having identified your anger, ask yourself: *Am I right to feel angry about this thing, or situation?* Picture the situation. Begin to understand why you react with anger. Ask your unconscious mind to show you the best way to deal with your anger. What would you like to change? (Shared laughter is a wonderful way of dissipating anger.)

5 Imagine talking the problem over and communicating your feelings with the person or persons involved. They may quite sincerely have no idea that their behaviour upsets you. Consider whether it is possible that you have misread or misunderstood the situation. See yourself using different responses so that the anger simply isn't there any more. Be prepared to forgive – no one is perfect, we can all makes mistakes, we can all be thoughtless sometimes.

6 Be still for a few minutes and enjoy the feeling that comes from this new awareness, or new understanding of yourself and your feelings.

7 Where your feelings of anger have nothing to do with an individual, see how best you can channel that energy. Sometimes an authority may make rules that infuriate you, but when it is impossible to do anything about a situation, anger is pointless. Change your focus to something positive where you can have an effect.

8 From now on, before getting angry, determine to pause first and consider whether anger would achieve anything positive or whether there is a better way of communicating your feelings. Then act in the best way possible to achieve positive results.

9 Count slowly backwards from five to one, open your eyes and return to full conscious awareness, feeling relaxed, calm and at peace.

Note: We can rarely change other people but we can change the way we perceive them and the things they say or do. Instead of seething with anger every time you return home and discover that the family has made a mess of the house – there are toys and clothes lying all over the place – you may choose to see it as a compliment. Understanding that the children are so secure in your love that they feel safe to be themselves – even if it is in an untidy way – is a wonderful diffuser. See it as evidence that you are not alone, and that there are lovable – though maybe sticky – arms waiting to hug you.

12

Constructive Use of Criticism

In almost all of us, our instant reaction to criticism is to defend ourselves. Before stopping to ask whether there is anything justifiable in the criticism or whether we can learn from it, we become angry and retaliate.

What Does Criticism Achieve?

It may be a way of someone venting feelings they cannot express in any other way. In this case we need to look at the message behind the words.

When a husband says: 'You're always out. Can't you ever stay home?', and the wife replies with: 'What about you? You're down the club three nights a week, aren't I entitled to my nights out?', he is trying (unsuccessfully) to convey to his wife that he would like her to spend more time with him. She sees it as an unfair accusation and so the criticism is expanded to cover almost anything.

If he had said, 'I miss you when you're not here,' she might well have replied, 'I miss you too when you're down the club.' And they may have found a way of sharing more time together; or they may have arranged to be away from home on the same nights.

Criticism is sometimes offered in a genuine way to try to help the recipient. Here it is important that it is seen in that light. Hard to do, but not impossible.

'Your hair looks a mess cut like that' is not likely to get the right response. Far better to suggest, 'Your hair really suited you when . . .' It is often the *way* in which criticism is offered that causes the defensive reaction.

And it seems okay for us to criticize ourselves or our families, but heaven help anyone else who does!

Criticism is Only Someone's Opinion

Let us remember that criticism is, after all, only someone else's opinion. We have the right to accept or reject it.

If criticism is being used as a form of attack, a way of getting at you, there are several ways of dealing with it.

- Simply walk away or ignore it.

- Turn it into a joke.

- Quietly ask, 'Why do you need to do this to me?' This is a stopper. If they are going to answer you, they have to pause and examine their intentions. Often criticism of another is a way of hiding the poor opinion they have of themselves.

When threatened, people will often attack by using criticism. Confirmed atheists, for example, may attack religious beliefs in an endeavour to convince themselves that they are right.

I witnessed this once as I listened to a man who, with what he firmly believed to be logic and reason, was attempting to destroy another man's beliefs with harsh criticism. Finally the 'believer' looked at him and asked: 'Why do you need to destroy my beliefs? What difference will it make to you?' There was a moment's silence, and then the atheist replied: 'None. I have no right at all. I apologize.'

One very common form of criticism concerns appearance. Most of us are sensitive about the way we look. This is never more so than when we are passing through those awkward years between childhood and adulthood. The young person has a desperate need to fit in, to be seen as 'one' with his/her contemporaries. This can cause parents to throw up their hands in despair. The good news is that these phases do pass. Withholding criticism of a teenage son or daughter usually indicates a caring and understanding attitude (appreciated by them even if they never tell you so!).

When people criticize physical things that can't be changed it is best to laugh at the person offering the unkind words, or to ignore them.

I recently read a story of a girl who was cruelly teased at school because she had large front teeth. She was taunted with names such as Goofy and Bugs Bunny. The news report, plus a photograph, showed the girl, now an adult, with the most wonderful smile. She was earning very high fees advertising toothpaste!

Constructive Use of Criticism

Examine the criticism. Is there any truth in it? Is it only another's opinion? Is it biased? Is this person feeling jealous or envious and allowing bitter, spiteful feelings to be expressed through criticism? Or is the criticism true? If so, how can you use it?

As a writer and artist I find criticism essential. Often I get so close to my work I can no longer see it objectively and I miss things that are important. I need an outside opinion. When criticism is offered, I listen, and then consider whether I can use it, or if it is correct. Sometimes I reject the criticism as not being true in terms of the way in which I want to present or portray something. I don't feel badly about this, a valid point has been made, it was an opinion I respected but I simply didn't see it that way. On the other hand, a fair criticism can be so helpful that to discard it out of hand would be a real loss.

Exercise 14 – Using Criticism Constructively

1 (You need only to be quiet, comfortable and relaxed to do this exercise.) Consider a criticism that has been made concerning you. One that bothers you – one that perhaps causes your mind to keep going back to it? Is it valid? Is it just someone's opinion? Or is it an attempt to communicate something else?

2 If you believe that the criticism is fair, see if there is any way in which you can constructively use it. Try to learn from it, or to use it in a way that enhances and strengthens that area of your life.

3 If the criticism is only an opinion, and yet you still feel upset by it, strengthen your ego. Build a good opinion of yourself. Say quietly to yourself: *I'm fine the way I am. I feel good about myself. Other people's opinions don't concern me.* Think for a few minutes of some of your good qualities – maybe you are kind, patient, trustworthy, industrious, a good listener . . .

4 Where you think that the criticism is an indirect way of telling you something else, decide how best you can deal with it. Perhaps, at a calmer moment, you need to talk with that person. Someone criticizing you for being too talkative, may really be trying to tell you that they want you to listen to them.

13

Motivation and Self-Discipline

Motivation

Why is it that some people are so motivated? They seem to have no problem at all in doing whatever they set out to do, while others flounder or never even get started?

How is it that some people can study, give up smoking, lose weight, start a new project and keep at it, where others only procrastinate or give up at the first hurdle?

Procrastinators talk endlessly about what they intend to do. They really *are* going to stop smoking next week, or the week after; they *will* send away for that book on yoga and make a start soon; they *are* going to paint the bathroom when they can get around to it.

What makes the difference and what can we do about it?

Let us look at what makes us get up in the morning (apart from needing to visit the bathroom).

When I ask this question, people come up with a variety of reasons: *I have to go to work . . . I need to get the children off to school . . . The neighbours will think I'm a lazy good-for-nothing if I stay in bed all day.*

The underlying reason is the same – fear. If they don't get to work on time they are likely to lose their job; if the children are habitually late the school attendance officer will be calling; and if they stay late in bed the neighbours may think badly of them.

Then there are the other reasons, and herein lies the clue. *I know my dog is waiting for me to take him out and he loves that early morning walk . . . I really enjoy that quiet half hour to myself before the rest of the family rise . . . I just love my job.*

The difference is in the way people view things. The first group see no pleasure in rising, they have nothing to look forward to; in truth they would probably rather lie in bed and avoid the day altogether. The second group have anticipation; there is something they are looking forward to doing. If we see something as really attractive, we are motivated to achieve that thing.

What if it is not attractive? Suppose the day starts with a pile of dirty washing to be done, or an unpleasant interview with the boss? The thought is always worse than the reality, for we do tend to blow things up out of proportion and imagine the worst.

The way to deal with procrastination, is to focus on the end result. The sooner the task is done, the sooner it is out of the way and you are free of it. Imagine having completed the chore – it must surely feel better.

'What do you mean, I put off doing things?'

To motivate ourselves, we should concentrate on the goal, not the chore. By doing this we strengthen our desire to do that thing. We may not want to spend two days decorating the bathroom, but if we keep before us a picture of how nice it will look when it is finished, we are motivated to persevere until it is completed.

Picturing four years of study to get a degree is daunting, but if you keep your goal in sight, enhancing it often by using your imagination, the task becomes easier.

Some things easily motivate us: meeting a loved one, going on holiday, collecting a new puppy, going out for a good meal. Here we are focusing only on the positives. We feel good about what we are going to do and can hardly wait for the event to arrive. Desire is a wonderful motivator.

By taking this approach and applying it to all areas where you have previously put off doing things, you can move from the negative end of the scale to the positive.

When a pending examination seems a long way off you may feel little motivation to get on with your studies. This is because the images you hold of taking that exam are too far off on your 'future' visual side. By bringing the imagined pictures of yourself sitting that exam in front of you when you think of it, you will be surprised how differently you feel about studying.

I recall a very successful business man who worked on a three- and five-year plan. When he explained how he dealt with his job, his hands indicated what was going on unconsciously inside his head: the three-year plan was kept right in front of him all the time, and the five-year one above and just a little further back. But both were kept in front of him whenever he thought about them.

Take a few minutes now and do the following visualization.

Picture something you have been putting off doing . . . Notice where you placed it. Most likely it was off-centre, perhaps even way off to one side. Now bring the image right in front of you and think about it . . . This prompts you to accomplish that thing. It feels more immediate – as if you really want to get on with it. By moving the image in front of you when you think about your project/goal, you are motivating yourself to get it done.

Survival and Motivation

We can't avoid the forces of procreation and self-preservation – they keep popping up. But self-motivation, for most of us, is not a natural response.

When we look at the animal world we see that they are motivated only by instinct – the instinct to survive. They hunt when they are hungry, search for shelter when it is necessary, and pursue a mate to ensure continuation of the species. Even play between animals is not a wasteful thing; they are learning, especially when young, as they test their strength and develop skills ready for when they are confronted by a life-threatening situation.

For most of us, the days of hunting in order to survive have disappeared. We do a job of work that indirectly provides food, shelter and clothing, and if that fails we have a State Benefit System. Personal drive, that motivation which used to exist in us, is for many no longer necessary.

To occupy ourselves we have invented activities such as sport, hobbies, study, and watching television. But as these are not essential to our survival, we have to motivate and discipline ourselves. Motivation outside survival is not natural. It is an attitude of mind we have to develop.

Facing Fears

Another reason for not doing things, is the fear of failure. If you never attempt something you do not have to deal with the feeling of having failed. In reality, the only failure is in not doing. To attempt something is to gain experience; even if you are not able, for whatever reason, to achieve your highest goals, you can feel good about yourself because you did, at least, try. In so doing, you learned, not only about the subject, but also about yourself.

Self-Discipline

Self-discipline goes hand-in-hand with motivation. It really is so much easier to give up than to pursue something that is difficult or demanding. To motivate yourself you need to increase your desire. You do this by focusing on all the positive aspects of achieving or doing that particular thing.

'Take one day at a time' is, in some respects, very sound advice. To contemplate months of denial and the effect upon your nerves and temper from giving up smoking, is enough to make you quit at the onset. Giving up smoking one day at a time seems less drastic. It may be far easier this way than contemplating the next 20 years without a cigarette. Do not focus on the struggle but on the achievement. Focus on all the positive aspects of being a non-smoker. (I knew a man who, with the money he saved when he gave up smoking cigarettes, bought a kit and built himself a sports car.) Use positive visualization often to help strengthen your resolve.

It is far easier to discipline yourself if you can see the task in a favourable light. Training for a sport can be gruelling and boring, but by focusing on small achievements – on your daily progress – you encourage yourself along, while still keeping your ultimate goal in view.

Learning and Re-Stimulation

Learning something new can re-stimulate bad experiences from childhood – especially school days. If you had a teacher of mathematics who terrified you, it is very likely you didn't do well in that class. As an adult, having to learn something related to maths can instantly bring back those negative feelings. They may be so unpleasant that you back off. You find you can't concentrate, or your mind goes blank. But the truth is that you weren't hopeless at maths, you just had a bad teacher.

When we are happy we learn best. In a state of anxiety the brain cannot function properly. If only teachers realized this, we would see the percentage marks in class go shooting up.

The secret to motivation is in the strength of our desire to do something. Avoid thinking about possible failure.

Exercise 15 – Motivation

Note: Having completed some of the previous exercises you should now find that you can quickly and easily reach alpha level. If you would like to use a quick induction use the one already given in Exercise 13 or choose one from the list at the back of the book. You would then go on to step 3 of this exercise.

I have found that many people still like to go right through a relaxation technique before beginning to deal with a problem. If this applies to you, proceed with the following induction.

1 Make yourself comfortable, close your eyes and relax. Imagine yourself in a hammock, or a rocking chair, or on a boat rocking gently at anchor. Create a picture of

yourself where you can imagine yourself moving gently to and fro, to and fro ... Breathe quietly in and out, and for a few moments concentrate on your breathing ... Imagine soft music playing in the distance, lulling you into a more and more deeply relaxed state ...

2 Feel your body relax. Notice how relaxed your toes feel. You can hardly feel some of them at all ... Let all of the muscles in your legs relax and as they do so, notice the feeling of heaviness in your legs as you relax deeper and deeper ... Now let your stomach muscles relax, feel how soft and warm and comfortable your stomach feels as you allow those muscles to relax. And as you sink down deeper and deeper you can feel the place where your head is resting, you feel the gentle pressure behind your back, beneath your bottom and the backs of your thighs as you let go and relax. Let all of the muscles in your scalp and forehead relax. Allow a calm, peaceful expression to pass across your face. Feel your eyelids relax. Let them go on and on relaxing until they feel so heavy, so comfortable, and so relaxed that you feel you just don't want to open them ... Let your mouth and lips relax ... Now let any stress or tension from your head, neck and shoulders, flow down through your arms and out through the tips of your fingers, and as you do so your arms feel so heavy, so heavy and so comfortable as you let go and relax ... Notice now your own physical signals telling you that you are completely relaxed – at alpha level.

3 Think about something you want do, or something that you ought to do but have been putting off. Make it something you can accomplish – not too difficult or too ambitious at first. Why do you want to do it? What will it achieve for you? How will you feel when you have done this thing?

4 Decide when you are going to start. Set an exact time. The day, the hour that you will begin . . . Decide where you will be when you begin and how you are going to proceed . . . Visualize yourself doing this thing. The more energy you create by thinking positively about your goal, the more you will help strengthen your own desire to act.

5 Relax for a few minutes and picture your goal . . . See yourself working towards it . . . See yourself succeed.

6 Count slowly backwards from five to one, open your eyes, have a good stretch and return to full conscious awareness with a wonderful feeling of confidence and belief in your own ability to reach every goal that you set for yourself.

Note: By following through and actually doing this particular thing, you are building a structure on which all future motivation can be moulded. You may repeat this exercise as often as you need.

14

Sleeping Well

There are few things more likely to get people down than sleepless nights, or struggling hour after hour to get to sleep. When all the world around you seems at rest, time drags by with excruciating slowness.

Why is it that some people find it so difficult to go to sleep? There are several reasons (excluding pain), but they all add up to the same thing – when the brain is alerted by thoughts going round and round in your head, it prevents you from sleeping. When you stop thinking in words (unless you are involved in meditation of some kind) you go to sleep. But how do you stop those thoughts? Often they are so futile, so unimportant, that it seems ridiculous they should have such an influence.

Sleep is in many ways a habit. It is, for most people, necessary to have a certain number of hours each night in order to function effectively.

The first thing to accept is that if you do have a bad night, or even several, nothing serious is going to happen to you. During the last war, with air-raids and the need to work night-shifts, people learned to survive on far less sleep than they had previously thought possible. However, we are individuals with our own needs, and those needs do vary. Most people do not need more than eight hours sleep, some do very well on as few as four hours a night.

It is the quality of sleep that is important. Four hours of deep sleep can be more beneficial than ten hours of restless tossing and turning.

To sleep well, it does help to take some physical exercise and fresh air during the day. You need a bed that is comfortable and placed in a draught-free position. Your clothing should be light and non-restrictive. You should also avoid eating late at night. All these points may sound like plain common sense, but it is surprising how often they are overlooked.

Some people believe they can only sleep when all is quiet. But most of us can get used to trains passing in the night or church bells chiming every quarter. If noise is a real bother to you, use positive suggestion at alpha level to tell yourself that you can ignore any noise you recognize as being safe and normal. The unconscious mind is ready to awaken you if there is a real threat, you don't need to have 'one ear cocked'. Sometimes the unconscious mind needs to be told that!

One of the most common causes of not sleeping well is worry. As you allow the conscious mind to relax, thoughts kept at bay while you have been occupied will come crowding in, and it seems impossible to stop them. Using Exercise 7, put all the stress-related things into the casket and drop it down the well. Then wander through your garden, really exploring it and adding to what you find there. As you do this, allow yourself to drift down into your natural sleep.

It may help to keep a pad and pencil beside the bed and write down any thoughts or things you need to remember or to deal with the next day. After doing this, relax, and picture a pleasant scene such as a walk in the country or on a beach, to help you drift down into a deep, satisfying sleep.

To push out niggling, fruitless thoughts, concentrate on something pleasant that is in no way stressful. You may go back to a childhood haunt, a previous house or garden, a holiday memory – enhance it with sounds, touch, smells, or tastes where appropriate. If you find your mind drifting back to those nagging thoughts, firmly pull it back to the good memories and pleasant scenes.

This is much like using one of the techniques described to reach alpha level. By giving yourself something specific to focus on, you prevent other thoughts from intruding. And because the exercise is not important or essential, the Left Brain gets bored with it and begins to relax, allowing the Right Brain to take over. You drift through alpha level to theta level and you are asleep.

Should you wake up in the night, don't start to worry about getting back to sleep. Use the same method to concentrate on something pleasant and restful, and try to go right into that experience.

'So! You have problems sleeping.'

Recording some of the exercises onto cassette and then listening to them as you relax and go to sleep works very well for some people. I sometimes meet clients years after treatment has been completed who tell me that they still, from time to time, pull out the cassettes I made for them and use them when they feel stressed or are having difficulty in getting to sleep.

If you have a long history of sleeping badly, you may need to break the habit. To do this, go to bed one hour later each night – if your normally go at ten, go at eleven, and then the next night at twelve, and so on. This may need to be done over a week when you do not have to go to work, but this method often breaks the habit. Once you have completed a cycle and reached what is, for you, a reasonable time for going to bed, try from then onwards to keep as near to that time as possible.

Bear in mind that some people do not need much sleep. You may simply be one of them. For myself, I have discovered over the years that I get by very well with only sleeping every other night. As I said, we are all individuals with our special needs!

In Conclusion

We've come a long way together since you began this book. If you have used some of the exercises already I am sure you will have begun to get results.

On looking back over my manuscript, the message that keeps coming through, above everything else, is that our ability to make changes – to enhance, limit or spoil our lives depends on the pictures we create in our minds.

In Conclusion

Appendix

Now as the swing breathing deeply and evenly

Exercises Leading to Alpha Level

Note: Always commence an exercise by placing yourself in
a comfortable, relaxed position, knowing that you have
time to complete the session without interruption.

The first six exercises have already been described in the
main text of the book. They are repeated here for you to
use in circumstances other than those given in detail in the
various chapters.

Using a Swing

1 Gently close your eyes and take a deep, deep breath;
really fill your lungs with air then breathe out and relax
. . . Continue breathing deeply and evenly, and as you
do so notice any jerkiness or unevenness in your breathing and try to smooth it out . . .

2 As you continue breathing deeply and evenly imagine
that each breath you take in is like a swing going up into
the air, and as you exhale the swing comes back down
again . . .

3 Mentally create your surroundings. Your swing can be
in any place you choose: in a familiar garden or one from
your own imagination; it can be in a park or tied to a
tree in an old orchard . . . You may like to imagine you

are a child again sitting on the swing, or perhaps you prefer to be pushing someone else ... As you continue breathing deeply in and out, imagine what you can see as you look up ... a clear blue sky overhead with an aeroplane high above you, its wings shining silver in the sunlight. Perhaps you hear birds or the sound of children's voices as they play. As the swing goes up you may be able to see over the treetops or rooftops and you may see a church spire in the distance ...

4 Now as you continue breathing deeply and evenly, notice any physical discomfort: it may be in your lower back, in your neck, or your shoulders ... When you have located it, calmly acknowledge it ... and as you continue to breathe deeply in and out, imagine that you are feeding oxygen directly to that area – life-giving oxygen, cleansing and healing – and as you breathe out you release any stress or tension, you just let it melt away ...

5 Continue in this way for a few minutes until you feel comfortably relaxed, and then begin to mentally check over your body, starting with your feet. Think of each toe in turn, first on one foot and then on the other ... By now you will notice that you have become so relaxed that you can hardly feel some of your toes at all and that you can barely distinguish one toe from the next ... Be aware of the feelings of heaviness in your legs as you let go and relax. Let them feel heavy, so heavy, so comfortable and so relaxed. That's fine, just let every muscle go on and on relaxing as you continue checking over your body ... Feel your stomach muscles relax as you breathe gently in and out ... Notice the rhythm of your breathing ... it has slowed down and that's perfectly natural, the same thing happens each night as you go to sleep ... You may even be able to feel your heart beating as you relax, deeper and deeper. Let your scalp relax, allowing all of the muscles in your face, your mouth and lips to

relax. Let the muscles in your neck and shoulders feel soft and relaxed . . . Imagine all the stress and tension from your head, neck and shoulders flowing down your arms and out through the tips of your fingers . . . Notice how your arms begin to feel so heavy, so heavy and so comfortable as you let go and relax . . . Notice now the feelings and sensations in your hands and fingers . . . Be aware of any tingling, any throbbing of pulses, any warmth or coldness . . .

6 Be still and breathe quietly . . . Be aware of your own feelings . . . Each one of us experiences this level of relaxation – the alpha level – in our own way. For some it is a feeling of great heaviness in the legs, or arms, or in the body. Others experience a weightless floating sensation; you may feel that your feet are numb or you may experience a tingling sensation. You are simply learning to recognize total relaxation and with practice you will be able to achieve this state quickly and easily. In this lovely relaxed way you begin to recognize your own feelings and sensations. Note these physical signals for they tell you when you have reached the level of relaxation necessary for positive instructions and suggestions to be received by your unconscious mind. Once you recognize these signals, proceed with your self-hypnosis suggestions and visualization.

Your Own Special Room

1 Gently close your eyes, relax and imagine yourself in a beautiful room that you have created. You had all the money you needed to make this room warm and comfortable. There is an open fireplace with a crackling log fire in the hearth; some photographs or pictures hang on the walls; there is a bowl of flowers on a polished

coffee table – you notice the colour of the flowers – you may even be able to smell the faint perfume from them. You sit in a comfortable armchair in front of your fire and relax . . .

2 Pay attention to the feelings and sensations in your body as you let go and relax. Check the feelings in your toes, your feet and your leg muscles as you let go and relax. Feel your stomach muscles relax . . . Notice the rhythm of your breathing as you let go and relax . . . Your breathing will have slowed down and that's perfectly fine, the same thing happens each night as you go to sleep. Allow a calm, peaceful expression to pass across your face as you relax all of the muscles in your scalp and forehead. You can feel your tongue resting comfortably inside your mouth as you let your lips and mouth relax. Now let the muscles in your neck and shoulders relax. Imagine all the stress and tension from your head, neck and shoulders flowing down your arms and out through the tips of your fingers. Notice the feelings in your hands as you relax deeper and deeper into your own natural state of alpha level. Proceed with your own suggestions and visualization.

In a Garden

1 Make yourself physically comfortable and relax. Close your eyes and picture yourself going down ten wide stone steps into a beautiful garden. Breathe deeply in and out and count quietly to yourself as you go down each step . . . At the foot of the steps you pause and look around. What season is it? Notice the flowers, the shrubs, the sounds of birds. Perhaps you can see butterflies, a fish pond . . . Take your time to create a garden you can enjoy . . . Wander through your garden noticing

the texture of the path beneath your feet, the gentle warmth of the sun on your skin . . . Presently you come upon a seat where you can sit down and relax for a while.

2 Now check over your body, starting with your toes, then your feet, leg muscles, stomach, chest, head and face muscles, neck and shoulder muscles – imagine any tension flowing down through your arms and out through the tips of your fingers. Let your hands relax – feel yourself physically relax. Take your time, enjoy the experience of total, complete relaxation.

3 You begin to recognize your own physical signals telling you that you are totally relaxed, at alpha level. Perhaps for you it is a feeling of heaviness, a tingling or throbbing of pulses, a floating sensation. Once you recognize these signals, proceed with your self-hypnosis suggestions and visualization.

Counting Backwards From 500

1 Make yourself comfortable and relax. Look across the room and focus your eyes on something in front of you. Anything will do – a picture, a mark on the wall, a lamp . . . As you continue to focus on that spot, begin counting slowly backwards from 500 quietly to yourself . . . Continue counting until you feel your eyes getting tired and wanting to close. As soon as they feel ready to close, let them. Don't struggle to keep them open, they will naturally begin to feel tired or watery and start to blink. Let everything happen naturally.

2 When your eyes have closed, stop counting and mentally check that each part of your body is completely relaxed. Feel your toes relax, your legs, your body . . . Allow a calm, peaceful expression to pass across your

face; let your mouth and lips relax. Imagine all the stress
and tension from your head, neck and shoulders flowing
down your arms and out through the tips of your
fingers. Be comfortably aware of the feelings and sensations in your body as you relax to alpha level. Use your
own suggestions and visualization.

Using the Blackboard

1 Make yourself comfortable and relax. Imagine before
you a child's blackboard and easel. Several pieces of
fresh white chalk are resting on a ledge at the front of
the board. In a moment you are going to imagine yourself leaning forward and taking a piece of chalk in your
fingers. You begin writing on the blackboard, starting
with the first letter of the alphabet. When you have done
this, say the name of that letter quietly to yourself, then
erase the letter and proceed with the next one. Again
look at it, say it quietly to yourself, erase it, and continue
in this way through the alphabet until you reach the
letter Z . . . As you erase this last letter take a deep, deep
breath and as you breathe out feel yourself drift down
into your own natural state of alpha level. Notice your
physical signals as you let go and relax.

Continue as follows if you wish.

2 Imagine now that you leave your chair and open the
outside door. As you look out you see that it is a lovely
evening and you feel a great longing to go out for a
while. You put on comfortable outside shoes and a
lightweight jacket . . . It is springtime and as you walk
along you notice the fresh green leaves on the trees, the
delicate yellow primroses in the hedgerow. Birds are
chirping and there is the distant sound of an aeroplane

engine high above you in a clear blue sky. Presently you come to a beautiful woodland, safe and secure. You decide to walk through the wood . . . It is so quiet and tranquil here. The ground becomes soft under foot with years and years of fallen leaves. Sunlight is filtering through the leaves of the trees, coming down in shafts of light to touch the path before you . . . Soon you hear the sound of running water. You reach a lovely stream. The water is clear and sparkling and you pause, watching it ripple over the stones and pebbles. You find a comfortable place on the grassy bank and sit down beside the water. You can reach forward and place your fingers in the water and feel the fresh cool water running between your fingers. You feel at peace and relaxed.

3 Consider your problem. What is it that you want to change? Use positive suggestions and visualization.

Gently Rocking

1 Make yourself comfortable, close your eyes and relax. Imagine yourself in a hammock or in a rocking chair, or on a boat rocking gently at anchor. Create a picture of yourself somewhere where you can imagine yourself moving gently to and fro, to and fro . . . Breathe quietly in and out, and for a few moments concentrate on your breathing . . . Imagine a gentle relaxing sound, or soft music playing in the distance, lulling you into a deeper and deeper relaxed state . . .

2 Feel your body relax. Notice how relaxed your toes feel. You can hardly feel some of them at all . . . You let all of the muscles in your legs relax and they begin to feel so heavy, so heavy, so comfortable and so relaxed. You let

your tummy muscles relax. And as you sink down deeper and deeper you can feel the place where your head is resting. You feel the gentle pressure behind your back, beneath your bottom and the backs of your thighs as you let go and relax. You notice the rhythm of your breathing and you can feel your chest moving gently as you breathe in and out, in and out . . . Let all of the muscles in your scalp and forehead relax. Allow a calm, peaceful expression to pass across your face. Feel your eyelids relax. Let them go on and on relaxing until they feel so heavy, so heavy and so relaxed that you feel you just don't want to open them. Let your mouth and lips relax . . . Now let any stress or tension from your head, neck and shoulders flow down through your arms and out through the tips of your fingers. Your arms feel so heavy as you let go and relax . . . Notice now your own physical signals telling you that you are completely relaxed – at alpha level. Use positive suggestions and visualization.

You may also wish to try the following new exercises.

Visiting a Childhood Memory

With your eyes closed, imagine revisiting a house from your childhood – a place with happy memories. Open the door and go inside. Remember all you can about that house as you explore each room. Finally, choose a room where you want to stay a while and relax. Make yourself comfortable. Now, mentally check over your body, starting with your toes and feet . . . Recognize your physical signals telling you when you have reached alpha level. Then programme yourself with positive suggestions and visualization (or use an exercise that is appropriate to help you resolve your problem or achieve your goal).

On the Beach

With your eyes closed, imagine that you are on a lovely beach, walking over the soft warm sand with bare feet. Feel your feet sink in a little way, leaving imprints in the sand. As you look down you notice seaweed, shells, perhaps a gull . . . When you reach the water's edge you pause and look out across the sea, noticing the colour of the sky, any clouds that may be drifting there. You step a little closer to the water, feeling the gentle waves lapping over your toes. The water is so warm and pleasant that you may like to imagine yourself going in deeper. You may even take a swim if you choose. Remember, you can do anything with your imagination. Eventually you leave the water and walk back up across the beach, where you find a place to sit or lie down and relax. As you relax deeper and deeper, notice your own physical signals telling you that you are at alpha level. Proceed with positive suggestions and visualization or follow on by using a specific exercise.

The Secret Door

Close your eyes and picture a wall in front of you. In this wall there is a secret door leading to a special place where you can relax and be yourself. Create your surroundings – they can be real or fantasy. Notice what thoughts or pictures come to mind. Approach with interest and curiosity what is before you. Anything you discover here will have a special meaning – it may lie completely outside your conscious awareness and in this way will be of special value to you. Stay there until you feel something you needed to understand or complete has been accomplished. You will know when this has happened – there will be some kind of signal. This signal may come as a desire to move or scratch yourself, you may sigh deeply. Open your eyes and return to your everyday world.

From time to time you may choose to return through this door to allow your unconscious mind to work for you. When you have a problem you can't define or you want to let the creative part of you have freedom to develop, go through your door in the wall and explore. Be curious about what you will find there.

Note: All creative people do something similar to this. There is a time when the logical Left Brain must stand to one side and allow the Right Brain to take over.

A Different Way to Relax

Close your eyes. Place your hands comfortably in your lap or on the arms of your chair and relax. Concentrate on the little finger of your right hand. Try to be aware of the sensations in it: the length and thickness of that finger, any tingling or throbbing you experience. Picture the shape and colour of the nail. Still holding on to the awareness of all these sensations in that little finger, pay attention to the next finger in the same relaxed way . . . and now your middle finger . . . and now your first finger . . . and now your thumb . . . Notice the feelings in the palm of your hand: you may experience a tingling or throbbing . . . Notice now the back of your hand: be aware of the temperature of the air against your skin . . . Still holding on to the awareness of all those feelings and sensations in your right hand, go now to your left. Starting with the little finger of your left hand, notice any feelings or sensations in exactly the same way . . . Notice each finger in turn, then your thumb, the palm of your hand and the back of your hand. Concentrate on the feeling of weightlessness in your hands as you let go and relax. Stay with those feelings for a few moments and then picture a large balloon being tied to one wrist. Imagine it lifting your hand up into the air . . . If at this stage, your hand actually feels like floating, let it do so. When you have experienced this lovely weightless sensation, imagine cutting the string and let your hand float back down again. You will be at alpha level. Now use positive suggestions and visualization.

Self-Healing

The above induction is a good way to lead into visualization for self-healing. To continue, picture a beautiful healing light surrounding your whole body. It has a gentle warmth that is cleansing and healing. Be relaxed and peaceful. You have the capacity to heal yourself – if this were not true we could not have survived as a species. By relaxing and focusing on that part of your body in need of healing, you direct your natural healing energy to that area. See it as a good thing – picture a beautiful healing light helping your body to do what it naturally wants to do.

Return to this healing light and visualize it several times each day when you are ill. It can only do good. Visualizing in this way also helps strengthen your immune system.

The body 'wants' to heal itself. As you think about some past illness or injury from which you made a complete recovery, remember how you dealt with it mentally. You 'knew' it would get better. Use that same attitude towards any illness you may have now – *expect* to get better.

Note: Although self-healing is a subject that needs to be dealt with separately, I felt I could not complete this book without giving you a simple way of helping yourself to better health.

Further Reading

Bramson, Robert M and Harrison, Allen F, *The Art of Thinking*, Berkley Books, New York

Cleese, John and Skynner, Robin, *Families and How to Survive Them*, Mandarin, 1993

Cleese, John and Skynner, Robin, *Life and How to Survive It*, Mandarin, 1994

Dantes, Ligia, *Your Fantasies May Be Hazardous to Your Health*, Element Books, 1996

Field, Lynda, *The Self-Esteem Workbook*, Element Books, 1995

Frankl, Victor, *Man's Search for Meaning*, Hodder, 1994

Godefroy, Christian H and Steevens, D R, *Mind Power*, Piatkus, 1993

Grant, Wendy, *Dare!*, Element Books, 1996

Grant, Wendy, *How to be Lucky*, Eastbrook Publishing, 1994

Grant, Wendy, *You and Your Dreams*, Eastbrook Publishing, 1995

Gawain, Shakti, *Meditations*, New World Library, 1991

Hauck, Dr Paul, *How To Be Your Own Best Friend*, Sheldon Press, 1988

Meares, Ainslie, *Wealth Within*, The Hill of Content Publishing Company, 1994

Osho, *What Is Meditation?*, Element Books, 1995

Roet, Dr Brian, *All in the Mind*, Optima, 1994

Sheehan, Elaine, *Health Essentials: Self-Hypnosis*, Element Books, 1995

Zukav, Gary, *The Seat of the Soul*, Century, 1991

Index